The Victorian Household Album

THE VICTORIAN HOUSEHOLD ALBUM

Compiled by ELIZABETH DRURY
& PHILIPPA LEWIS

FROM THE AMORET TANNER EPHEMERA COLLECTION

C&B
COLLINS & BROWN

Frontispiece: Taking Tea, a painting by David Emil Joseph de Noter
(Bridgeman Art Library)

First published in Great Britain in 1995
by Collins & Brown Limited
London House, Great Eastern Wharf
Parkgate Road, London SW11 4NQ

1 3 5 7 9 8 6 4 2

British Library Cataloguing-in-Publication Data:
A catalogue record for this book
is available from the British Library.

ISBN 1 85585 221 7 (hardback)
ISBN 1 85585 232 2 (paperback)

Conceived, edited and designed by Collins & Brown Limited

Art Director: Roger Bristow
Editor: Catherine Bradley
Designed by: David Fordham

Filmset by Harrington & Co., London
Reproduction by Typongraph, Italy

Printed and bound in Spain

Contents

INTRODUCTION

As THE YEARS of Queen Victoria's reign rolled by there was hardly a town in Britain that did not grow in size. Market gardens and farms disappeared under neat terraces, avenues and roads. Landowners, whose country estates had previously been a convenient carriage ride from town, saw the houses encroaching on their rural views and retreated. In London, quiet villages such as Paddington, Acton, Islington, Hackney and Brixton became simply patches, desirable or otherwise, that together made up the great capital city.

The vast expansion in housing was a reflection of the growth of the Empire itself, and the increasing wealth of a manufacturing and industrial nation. This was proudly displayed at the Great Exhibition in Hyde Park in 1851, where nearly seven thousand British exhibitors showed an extraordinarily comprehensive range of goods, from large-scale machinery to penknives, to over six million visitors. Although such exhibitions, designed to increase trade and display the latest technological advances, were commonplace in the nineteenth century, this was the first exhibition to be truly international and was followed by similar events in Philadelphia, Chicago and major European cities. It also made the link between art and industry and demonstrated that textiles, furniture, metalwork – all the furnishings of the house, in fact – need no longer be bought from craftsmen, but were being made in ever greater quantities and

in ever greater ranges of design in the factories of Great Britain. So the population filled their new houses with as many of these new devices and products of Victorian ingenuity and invention as they could afford. The house, the furnishings, the clothes and the servants were all a proclamation of prosperity and status for a vastly extended middle class.

This was observed by Hermann Muthesius, a German diplomat who lived in England in the last decade of the century; he noted the English streaming 'into the rural areas, creating dwelling-places for individuals, making them little separate worlds and concentrating and incorporating all the comforts of life into them... The Englishman sees the whole of his life embodied in his house. Here in the heart of his family, self-sufficient and feeling no great urge for sociability, pursuing his own interests in virtual isolation, he finds his happiness and his real spiritual comfort.' Muthesius was also interested in the unvarying routine of English households: 'all households of similar economic standing are like one another as peas in a

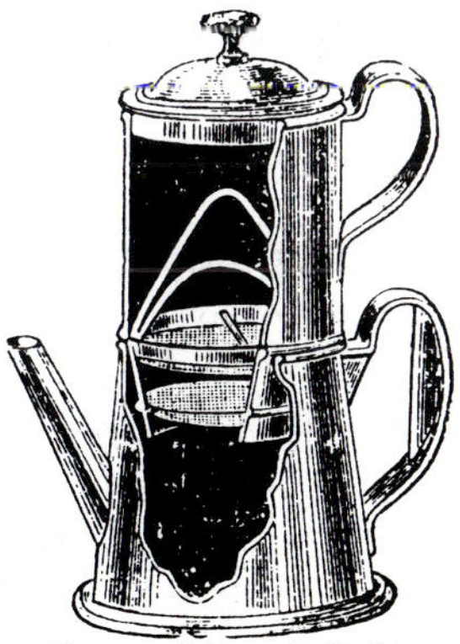
Improved French Cafetier.

"A Most Acceptable X-Mas Gift."

pod. They have exactly the same number of servants and the work is apportioned in exactly the same way, they have the same rooms, the same meals, the same daily routine for inmates.'

It was certainly the servants who supported the whole structure of the Victorian household, from the single maid-of-all-work in the modest terrace house to the large contingent behind the baize door of a grand country house. The time spent by the Victorian housewife on visiting, mastering the piano, inviting her friends to tea and

WRITING CASES.

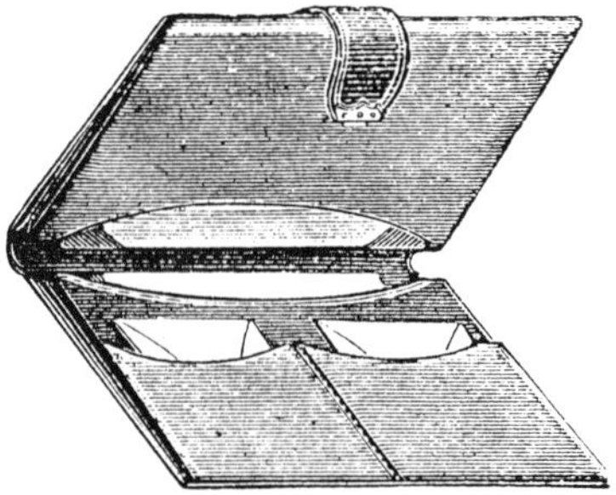

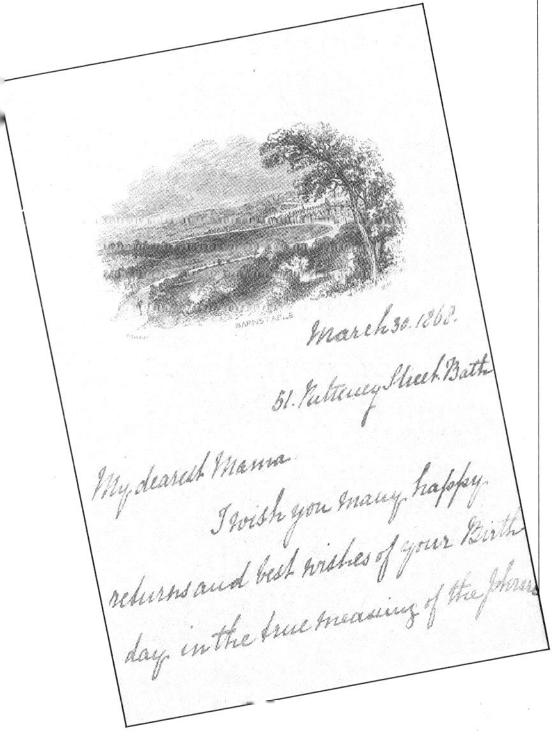
March 30. 1868.
51. Pulteney Street Bath

My dearest Mama

I wish you many happy returns and best wishes of your Birth day in the true meaning of the

creating trifles for charity bazaars was bought at the expense of servants, who performed the extremely labour-intensive tasks of washing, ironing, cleaning, cooking, lighting and warming the house and minding the children. The management of these servants was a not inconsiderable chore, and perceived as a problem of the age. Anne Cobbett's comments in 1842 were these: 'When she is fitting up her house, a young lady should consider the number, and the sort of servants she can afford to keep, and to regulate the style of the house accordingly...China, plate, pictures and all ornamental furniture, require peculiar nicety; and the dusting and polishing of them must be repeated daily, or they will bring discredit, not upon the servants, but upon the mistress of the house.' Years later, in 1889, Mrs Haweis wrote, 'In wrestling with domestic dangers and difficulties, it is impossible long to escape the vexed question of the day, or to blink the difficulty that lies far ahead of the rest, and that is – servants... Servants must come, and servants must go.'

A comfortable but servant-less house was unimaginable in the nineteenth century, but although some aspects of housekeeping did become easier as the century progressed, with packaged foods, cleaning materials and ready-to-wear clothes becoming readily available from the new department stores, the greatest innovation of all was a distant glimmer. Mrs Panton suggested in 1888 that her readers 'pray heartily for that bright day to dawn when electric light shall be within the reach of all, and when Mr Swan tells us how to light our houses as perfectly as he has done his own; and I confess that when I recollect that charming abode, where fairies seem to superintend the lighting, so wonderfully is it managed, I feel consumed with rage and anger, to think that I was not born in a time when the electric light will be as much a matter of course as the present odious system of lighting by gas is.'

Inhaler (Portable).

TO POLISH A PIANO. – Saturate a piece of chamois leather in sweet oil, and apply carefully to every part. Then, with a dry leather, rub well, renewing the pieces as they become greased with the oil. It will require one hour, or even longer, of constant rubbing to give it the gloss desired. For walnut furniture, take three parts of linseed oil to one part of spirits of turpentine. Put on with a woollen cloth, and, when dry, rub with a similar cloth. The polish not only covers the disfigured surface, but restores the wood to its original colour, and leaves a lustre upon the surface.

TO CLEAN GLASS GLOBES – When the globes belonging to chandeliers have become very dirty with smoke they should be soaked in warm soda-water. Then add to the water a few drops of ammonia, and wash the globes with a well-soaped flannel. Rinse in clean cold water, and dry with a linen glass-cloth.

JAPANNING OLD TEA TRAYS – First clean them thoroughly with soap and water and a little rottenstone; then dry them by wiping and exposure to the air. Now get some good copal varnish, mix with it some bronze powder, and apply with the brush to the shabby parts. After which, set the tea tray in an oven at a heat of 212 or 300 degrees until the varnish is dry. Two coats will make it equal to new.

TO CLEAN GILDING brush off dust with a feather brush. Never wipe with linen, as it takes off and deadens gilding.

PLUSH GOODS, and all articles dyed with aniline colours, when faded from exposure to light, may be much improved by sponging them with chloroform.

CHAIRS AND SOFAS upholstered in leather last much longer if the leather is regularly revived with the following mixture. It cleans the leather, and, at the same time, softens it and prevents it cracking: – Take one part of best vinegar and two parts of boiled linseed oil, and shake well together. Apply a little on a soft rag, and afterwards polish with a silk duster or an old chamois leather. The leather of chairs should be as regularly and carefully polished as their woodwork.

SWEEPING CARPETS – Many find that the use of tea-leaves in sweeping light-coloured or delicately textured carpets leaves stains on the material. Bran, slightly moistened, or fresh cut grass, form a capital substitute; the former especially, not only gathering up all dust and dirt, but reviving the hues of the carpet.

AN ARTICLE MADE OF BRASS may be kept bright and free from tarnish if you will cover it with a thin coat of varnish made of bleached shellac and alcohol – which may be procured of a chemist.

TO BRIGHTEN GILT FRAMES – Take sufficient flour of sulphur to give a golden tinge to about one and a half pints of water, and in this boil four or five bruised onions, or garlic, which will answer the same purpose. Strain off the liquid, and with it, when cold, wash with a soft brush, any gilding which requires restoring, and when dry it will come out as bright as new work.

THE CELERY GLASS, with its bouquet of vivid green, is a bright attractive ornament on the dining-table. This plant is a great nervine, and those suffering from any nervous trouble are much benefited by a liberal use of it. It is also recommended for rheumatism, some authorities going so far as to say that when freely eaten it is a sure cure for this painful disease. Celery leaves will be found good for flavouring soups, when celery is out of market, if they are put into a pan and placed in the oven to dry; be careful not to allow them to burn, and when dry crumble them and place away in a wide-mouthed bottle, which must be kept closely covered.

At Home

THE FRONT DOOR

IT WAS THE view of Shirley Foster Murphy that 'The position and arrangement of the principal entrance to a house is a point of very considerable importance, being, as it were, the key-note to the whole.' He also laid down that the front entrance should be on the opposite side of the house to the drawing room, which

HALL DOOR FURNITURE.

"There are, literally, square miles of glass in every town of moderate size that would be covered with GLACIER Window Decoration if only the owners knew of its fitness, beauty, and durability."

Specimen Window Screen or Top made up of one copy No. 184 and two copies No. 190.

M'CAW, STEVENSON & ORR'S PATENT

GLACIER WINDOW DECORATION IS OF WORLD-WIDE REPUTATION.

If you wish to shut out disagreeable views, to tone down excess of light, to secure privacy where windows are overlooked, or simply to introduce the beauty of colour and form into the windows of

The Home, the School, the Church, or Institution,

use the Glacier designs. The combinations are endless; so that any window, of any size or shape, can be fitted in perfect taste.

Specimen Filling, for Gothic Windows, No. 170.

...ers, ...567.

Specimen Centre, No. 119; French (style, Henri II.).
Several hundred different subjects—Figure, Floral, Heraldic, or Pictorial.

SEE OTHER SIDE.

Specimen Ground Filling, No. 2111.

would then not be overlooked from the carriage-drive. This arrangement would provide a greater degree of privacy for the house's occupants and would also enable the servants to answer the door without crossing the path of visitors. A porch large enough for visitors to be set down from their carriages under cover was also a desirable feature in an uncertain climate.

A German visitor to Britain noted in great detail the characteristic front door: 'Everywhere in England there are knockers on the front doors of houses. A knocker was once the only means by which a caller could make his presence known; but nowadays the bell has in fact rendered it superfluous. Callers simply ring when it would seem too familiar to knock. But the postman always uses the knocker to announce his visit as he pushes the post through the letter-box into the house. With a little practice one can judge the importance of his delivery by the way in which he knocks: for printed matter one will simply hear a curt, disdainful fall of the knocker, a loud knock will signify a letter, and registered post and telegrams, for which the door must be opened, will be heralded by two large knocks.'

Coloured glass in the front door lights was considered essential for any house with a claim to an artistic interior. A wide variety of designs were available, including patterns in the gothic, floral or heraldic style.

Receiving Guests

RIGHT: Fashionable visiting costumes for October 1879.

A N ETIQUETTE book published in 1872 stated: 'It is to be hoped that visitors will refrain from bringing either dogs or children. The former are apt to do a great deal of mischief in overturning things . . . and the latter, besides often hearing much which they should not, are apt to make awkward remarks, and are often as mischievous amongst china and nick-nacks as the canine pet.'

Visits, it stated, 'were absolutely necessary, being in fact, the basis on which that great structure, society, mainly rests. It is a safeguard against any acquaintances which are thought to be undesirable.' The rules were clear: calling hours were between three and six o'clock and no calls should be paid before luncheon unless on a very dear friend. No formal call should be longer than quarter of an hour. Cards must be left: a lady should leave one of her own and two of her husband's on the hall table. If paying a call on foot, cos-

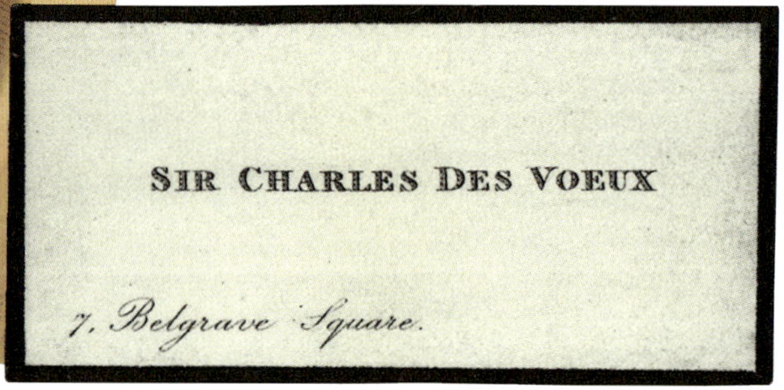

tume should be of a plain character, but if by carriage, handsome costumes made of rich silken materials, flowery or feathery bonnets and lace sunshades were suitable. The author's last words were reserved for gloves: 'When paying calls, gloves of a shade harmonizing in colour with the dress are usually worn.'

The Hall

The hall of a country house is conjured up in one household compendium as follows: it may 'rejoice in the sylvan trophies of the chase – antlers, the fox's head and brush – old carved oak cabinets may fill in recesses, and within them may repose collector's treasure. The carved oak chairs and table, the umbrella stands, the blazing open grate in winter, the same full of bunches of evergreens or large pots of hydrangea or azalea in summer, make it a pleasant place to linger in.'

Dealing with the confines of the hall of a town house, however, was considered far more problematic, and here there might only be space for the conventional type of table, seat and stand. The hall was agreed to be the social index of the house, and a great deal depended on how this important room was furnished.

Warmth was a keynote: *Home Notes* suggested that if it be 'prettily arranged with warm hangings and rugs, with the addition of a red dado to harmonize with the oriental hangings, it at once looks hospitable, and gives a bright welcome to all comers'. To prevent draughts and constant catching of cold, a double curtain of serge or felt could be hung on a portière rod over the front door. The idea that the hall might be a 'mere passage' was to be avoided by the addition of pictures and small tables with plants and books. One author advised having an illuminated card saying when the post went out, with a box underneath for letters, a timetable and a hat brush.

1939.

The Hall

A cast-iron umbrella stand manufactured by O'Brien, Thomas and Co., priced at 5/6d.

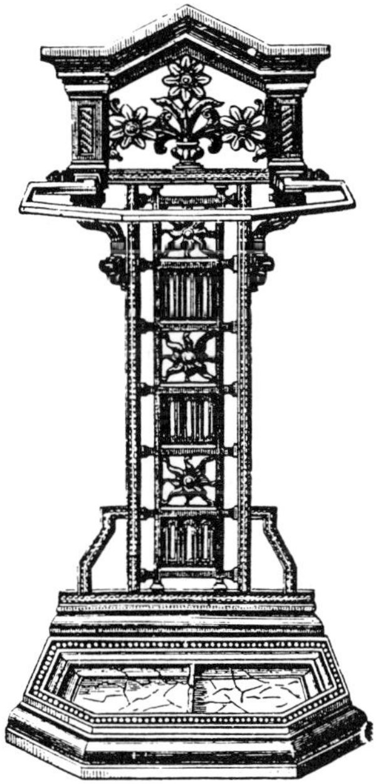

The Drawing Room

The drawing room was the 'best room', where, stated one author, 'fine manners are a necessity, and a certain amount of fine manners is maintained by use of a room that holds our dearest treasures and sees little of the seamy side of life. Small habits, such as changed dress for evening wear, the enforcement of the rule that slippers and cigars must never enter, and a certain politeness maintained to each other in the best room all give the proper drawing room air, and will go a long way towards keeping up the mutual respect that husband and wife should have for each other.'

Eunice, the decorating correspondent of *The Lady*, declared that 'the secret of a pretty room is to break up the straightness of the wall, and so arrange the chairs that they look as if a merry party of gossips had only just vacated them.' Another writer was of the opinion that the room must be in constant use: 'I am quite convinced that rooms resent neglect like human beings do, and that they become morose and sulky-looking if they are kept closed or opened only when strangers are expected.'

The pitfall of having too much furniture was illustrated by an anecdote of a guest standing to take a lady in to dinner and knocking over a chair, thus entangling his coat button in a fringed antimacassar. To disentangle himself he stepped back into a table, from which he knocked a book,

A table cover illustrated in the Young Ladies' Journal, *April 1888, to be made in olive felt, wool chenille and tinsel.*

photographs and a flower-holder, smashing 'the whole concern'. Finally, he backed away from the scene into a whatnot. Therefore, it was recommended that nothing should be bought which could not be easily replaced or withstand wear and tear: 'for if a room is too grand to be lived in day by day, your acquaintances will put you down on the list of dull folks to be avoided'.

The Drawing Room

BELOW: A suggestion for the corner of a drawing room from The Cabinet Maker and Art Furnisher.

Music at Home

Most necessary to a young girl's education was the study of music, and once she had been received into society she was expected cheerfully to comply with requests to perform at a social gathering.

BELOW LEFT: Piano music for games, songs and dances to be played at musical entertainments.

LEFT: 'Recollections from my early musical days', an illustration from The Young Lady's Book.

MUSIC
AT HOME

At the evening party described in *Warne's Etiquette of the Dinner-Table*, the gentleman seated next to the lady who had been prevailed upon to sing, conducted her to the piano, turned over her music, and did not leave her side until she returned to her seat.

'A lady does not wait for silence, but begins when she is ready. If it is a vocal effort, she will probably find a hush suddenly pervade the room. A "piece", however brilliantly executed, will, on the other hand, generally form the signal for conversation. Of this she will take no notice, but play on to the end, receiving the expression of thanks from those who have not heard a note with as pleasant a face as if they had paid her all the attention possible.'

'A kindly disposition and willingness to oblige will satisfy even the most censorious', the young performer was advised.

BELOW: Besides the 'Grand March', the book contained music for the 'Banjo Lancers', 'The Derbyshire Ram' and the 'Fairy Wedding Waltz'.

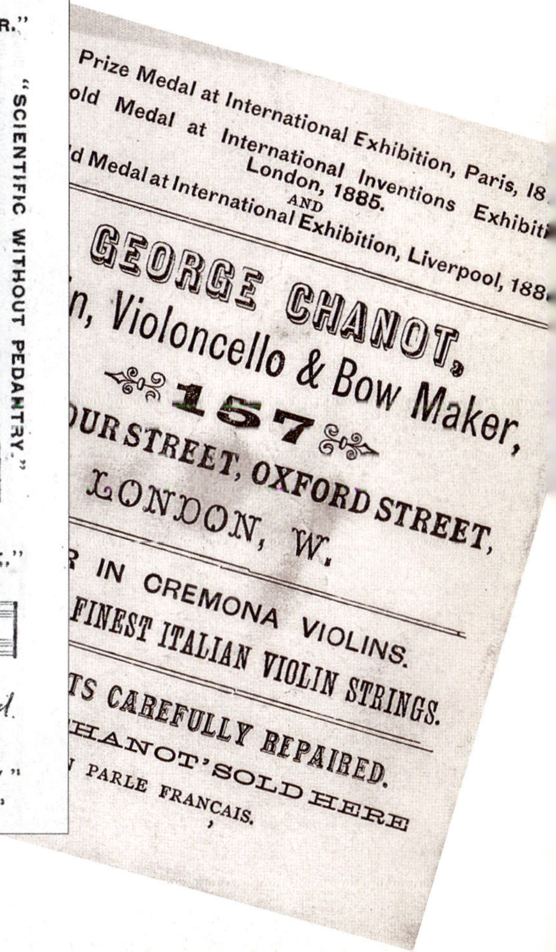

Dances & Balls

It was said that 'The requisites for an agreeable ball are a good room, good music and a good supper. It is of all entertainments the most extravagant.' The *Ball Room Guide* elaborated on these words: the fare should be liberal, but not vulgarly profuse: hot soup, fowls, ham and tongue, and whatever can be iced should be served in that way. If it were to be a ball of any pretensions, champagne should be provided, although no lady should partake of

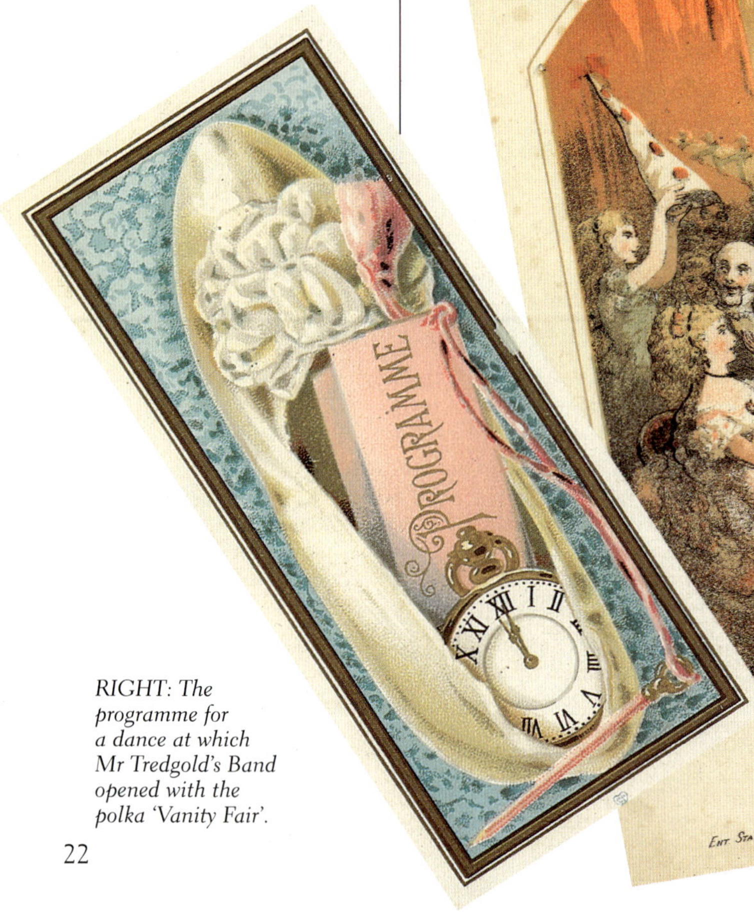

Lancers' Quadrilles.

1.—Top lady and bottom gent. chassez to the right. Swing round with right hand into place. Top couple lead through the bottom couple—return, leading outside. Four gents. right hand in centre, and set. Turn the ladies into the centre, forming grand cross. Ladies turn round to left, while the four gents. single dance the reverse … outside—turn partners.

…couple advance and retire twice, leaving the …t of opposite gent.; chassez to the right …ving to place. Top and bottom couple …allancez, and turn corners; advance and …, and turn partners to place. …dvance and stop; bottom gent. ad…tte and retire. The four ladies join …s in centre at the same time giving their … their partners' left hands; all dance round …orm of a double cross. Each gent. turn their …tners round to left into their places.

4.—Top couple with the lady at the left advance and retire twice; move to the lady on the right, and then to the lady on the left; three piourette; hands … round to place.

5.—Grand Chain. Top couple … The other couples do the sa… eight, ladies in front … side and gent… retire …

RIGHT: *The programme for a dance at which Mr Tredgold's Band opened with the polka 'Vanity Fair'.*

more than one glass. Advising on dress, the *Guide* stated that for elderly ladies a rich brocade 'and a somewhat profuse display of good jewellery' was permissible, but that young, unmarried ladies should wear dresses of the lightest possible material, such as net, tarlatane, gauze or muslin, over a delicate silk slip.

Programmes were given to each guest on arrival, so that gentlemen could engage their partners for each dance. 'Gentlemen should endeavour to entertain the ladies who dance with them with a little conversation, on something more novel than the weather and the heat of the room; in round dances they should be particularly careful to guard them from collisions and to see that their dresses are not torn,' exhorted the *Ball Room Guide*. It stated that a ball should commence with a quadrille, followed by a waltz. Polkas, mazurkas and schottisches 'may be thrown in as an occasional relief in the country, just as a country dance is often tolerated as a finale'.

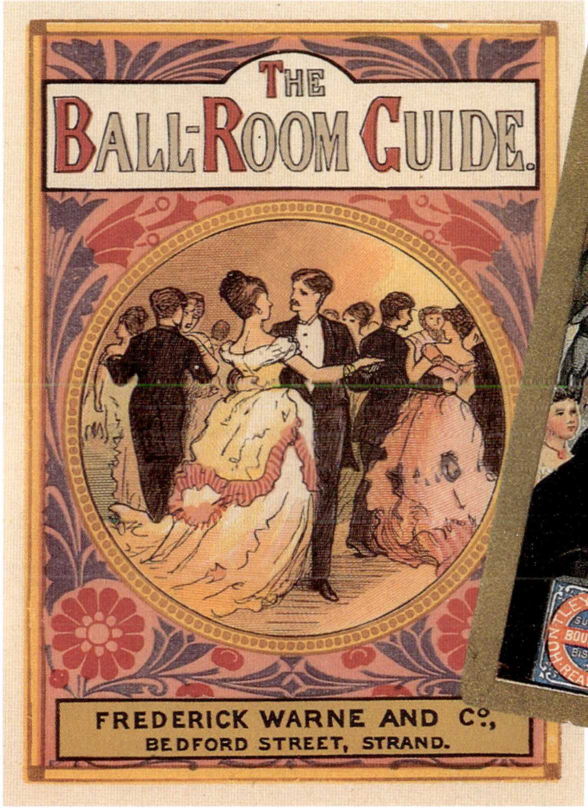

An advertisement for biscuits made by Huntley and Palmers, suppliers to Queen Victoria.

CURTAINS & BLINDS

The Window Blind Company also advertised improved fittings for roller blinds with a 'patent spring pulley rack'.

A PROPERLY dressed Victorian window needed to have a blind or muslin curtain to veil the bright sun, as well as a heavier draped curtain. 'A pair of beautiful and artistic curtains will at once raise an indifferently furnished room out of the commonplace', wrote Eunice of *The Lady* magazine. She advocated cretonnes for summer months, to be replaced in winter with heavier, warmer draperies in darker colours that were less prone to show the sooty dust from the

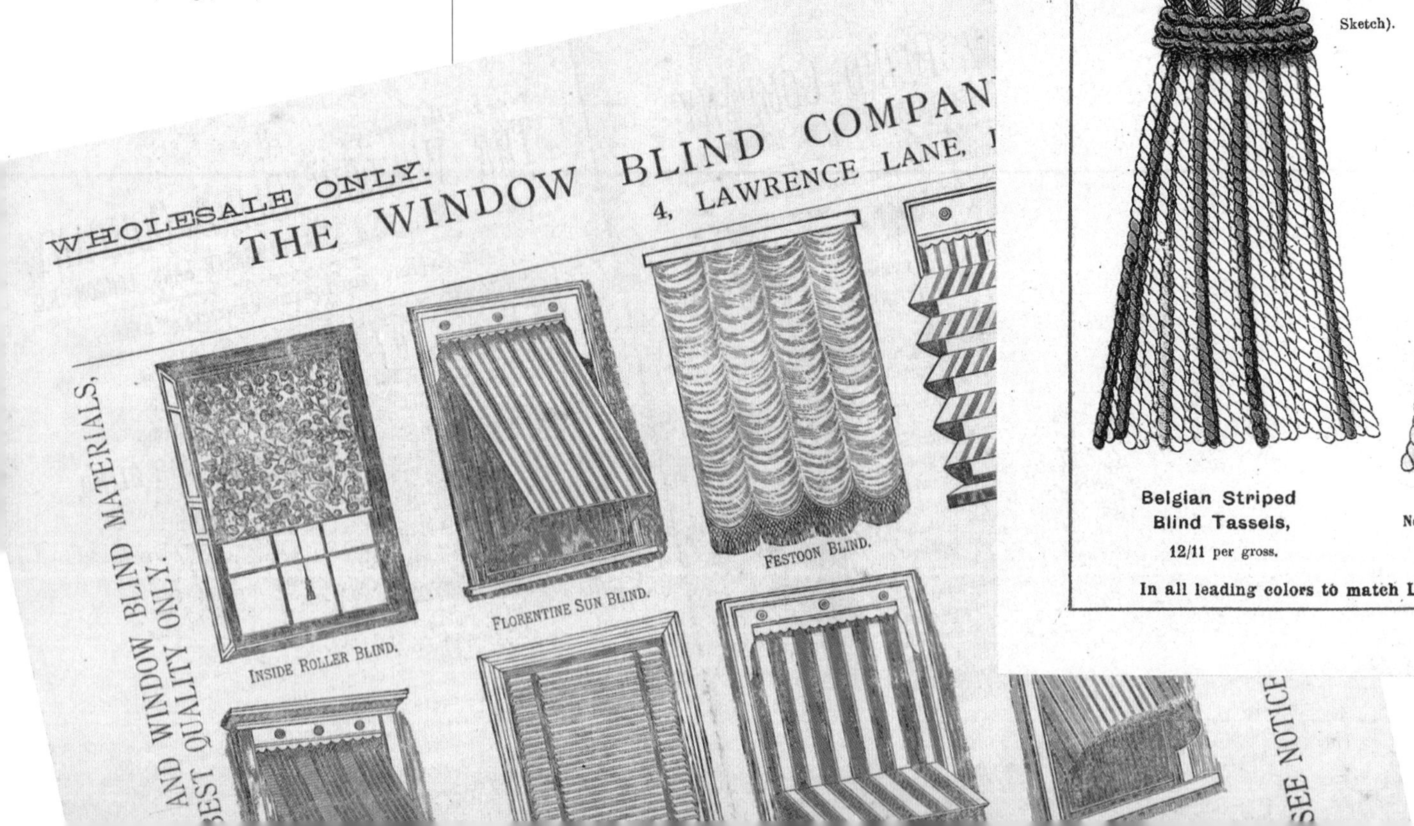

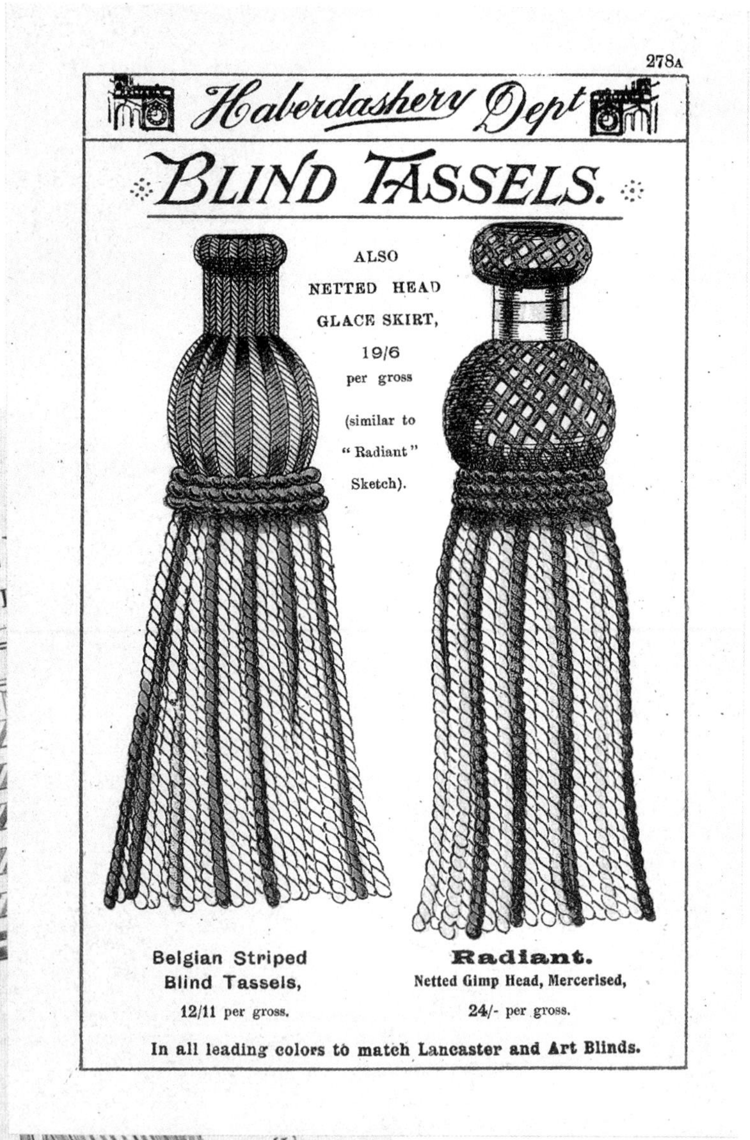

constant fires. Serge, which could be obtained in any colour to harmonize with the rooms, she described as 'not inartistic', but Friesland velvet was slightly dearer and 'really handsome in reception rooms, and I can thoroughly approve the gold, sapphire and moss green shades'.

Fifty years earlier Mrs Loudon had considered that crimson silk damask was far the best foil to feminine beauty, and correct for the drawing room 'with a piped valance or very deep gold fringe, and the inner muslin curtains should be trimmed with silk fringe of the same colour as the outer curtains'. Blinds were criticized as being dull in comparison with the glorious effect of light streaming through lace.

CURTAINS & BLINDS

RIGHT: Huntley and Palmers also offered Reading Shortbread 'of rich quality and attractive design, suitable for Afternoon Tea'.

MARKET-PLACE, Sleaford 1849

Mr Allen

BOT OF W. W. MASTIN,
Wholesale & Retail
Grocer, Tallow Chandler
& SEEDSMAN
Teas warranted Genuine as Imported.
Foreign Fruits, fresh roasted Coffee, Spices, Hops, &c.

1849 Feb 14 1 ¼ Sco Snuff 5/8
18 2 ¼ Do 5/8
March 16 2 ¼ Aroma 8
23 1 ¼ Do 20
31 1 Pk Oatmeal 20 1 – 8
Apl 4 2 Pks Do 20 4½

THIS IS 'the hour for confidential revealings that break into shy utterance as the light of the lamp and candles glimmer out upon the fading day. Above all, is it not the supreme moment when woman meets woman for the discussion of their fellow-beings?' Tea-time gossip was thus described by Constance Cary Harrison, who intimated in her book, *Woman's Handiwork in Modern Homes*, that showing off one's china was also part of the procedure: 'There is no limit to the range of our tea-tray collections: they embrace Davenport and Longwy, Crown Derby and Ming, Tokiyo and Dresden, Minton, Spode and Copeland, Sèvres and Etruria. Cups and saucers of every age and family meet together in the symposia of today. And sweeter far than honey of Hymettus is the draught of Chinese nectar sipped by a collector in the sight of china loving friends, from a fragile cup of which she knows no duplicate.'

Equal consideration was given to the tea-table itself and the quality of the tea-cloth. One writer advised on the purchase of a rush and bamboo table with little trays that opened and closed for the cakes. For the cloth, a fine white damask edged with torchon lace and marked with a large monogram in scarlet thread was recommended as washing beautifully.

Housekeeping manuals gave more precise instructions on how to organise this 'very popular form of entertainment, though more favoured by ladies than gentlemen'. Frederick Warne explained that for small friendly teas the ladies of the house, not the servants, would dispense the tea, that only tea cakes and bread and butter should be served, and that there should be no entertainment beyond conversation. Carriages should be kept waiting at afternoon teas, for ladies frequently remained for only a quarter of an hour.

At teas for fifty or more, Warne recommended serving tea and coffee in urns, as well as sherry, champagne or claret cup, ices, fancy biscuits, cakes and potted game sandwiches.

BELOW: A packet for a few ounces of tea.

Puzzles & Riddles

The opening words of *Guess Me*, compiled and arranged by Frederick d'Arros Planche, were, 'It has often puzzled the cleverest of us to make out simple Riddles. Trifling as these Exercises for Ingenuity may be considered, wise men have not disdained to amuse their leisure hours by their manufacture.' The book contained six hundred and thirty-one different conundrums, among them, 'Why is it reasonable to suppose that tight-rope dancers are great favourites with the public? – Because their performance is always *encored* (on cord).'

It also contained enigmas – poetical, allegorical and original – palindromes, pictorial puzzles of various kinds, historical mental pictures and quotations and hieroglyphic proverbs. 'My *first* is the product of my *second*, and my whole is pleasant to romp in', ran a geographical charade. The answer was: 'Hayfield'.

Puzzles & Riddles

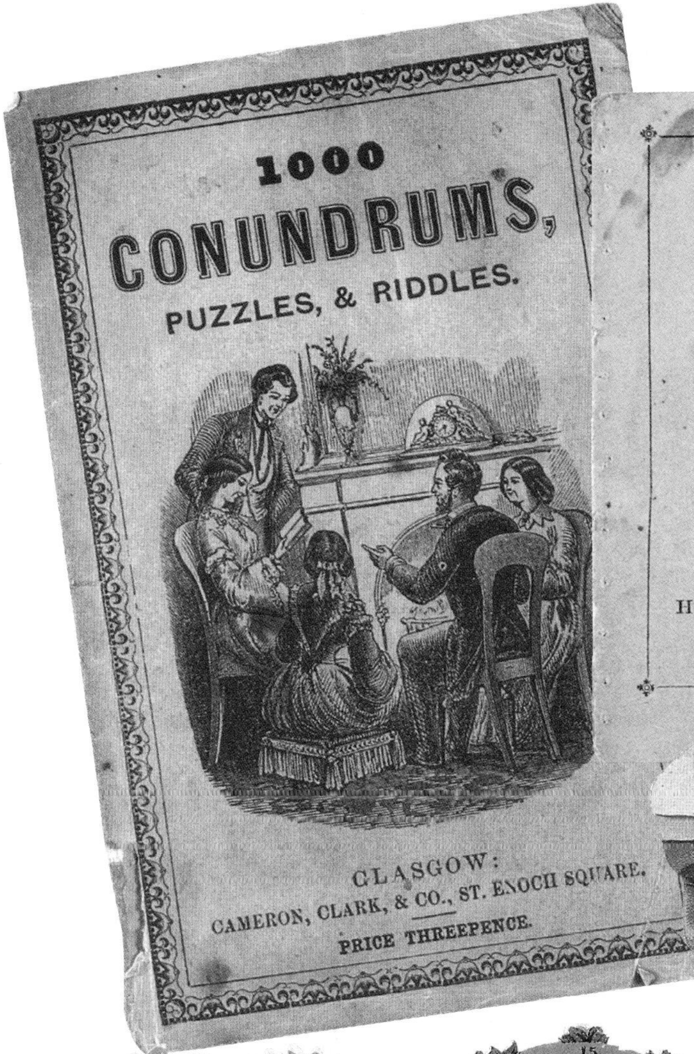

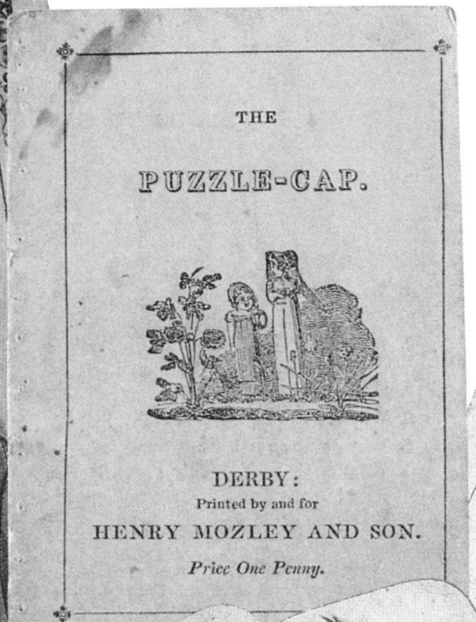

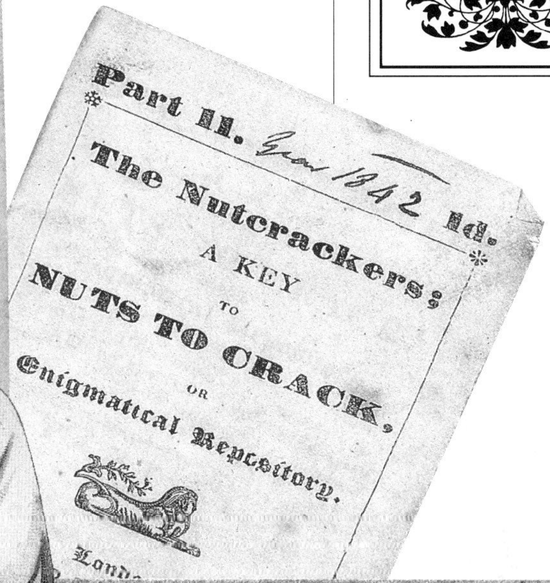

The Card Table

RIGHT: All manner of markers were produced for card games, the one made by Goddall & Son having a sliding indicator.

WHIST, BEZIQUE and cribbage were among the most popular card games played after tea on a winter's day or as after-dinner entertainment. The players sat round a table, generally covered by a green baize cloth, the markers required by the game before them.

To know the rules of such games was regarded as a necessary social accomplishment, and various books were published as guides for the beginner. *Whist*, in Warne's Bijou series, described the techniques of finessing ('throwing the enemy off their guard by passing a trick as though unable to take it') and revoking ('failing to play

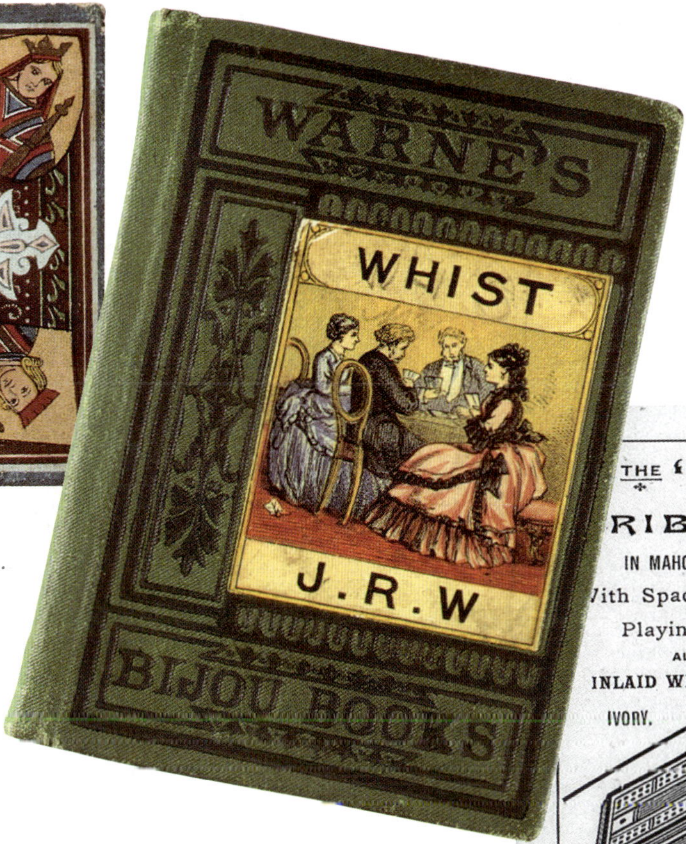

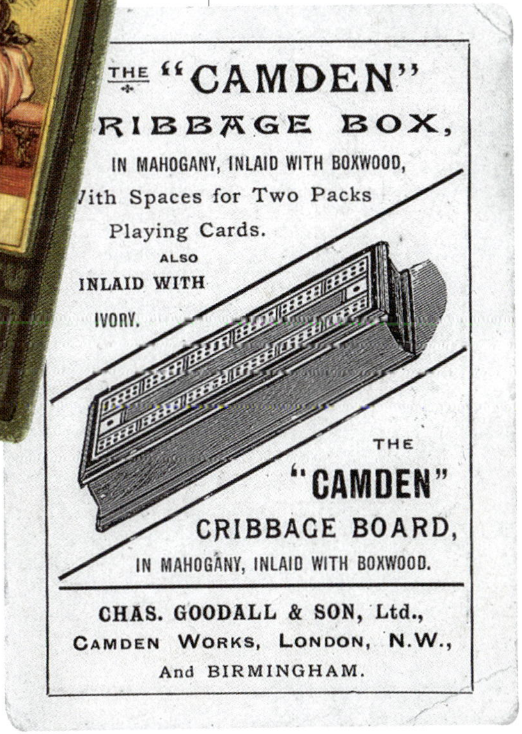

to a lead when you have cards of the suit led'), among others. 'By playing a straightforward game, you will most rapidly obtain the credit of being thought an intelligent whist player' was one of the axioms, and the book ended with the warning, 'Nothing at a whist table can be in worse taste or more vulgar than betting.'

Other Victorian card games, such as Muggins, My Rose Has Budded, Snip-Snap-Snorem (an 'excellent, mirth-producing round game'), did not call for any great exercise of the mental powers, admitted *The Popular Recreator*. General conversation could go unchecked, and it was thus 'eminently a social game, and often a very merry and agreeable one'.

The Morning Room

The morning room was the private sitting room of the lady of the house. Here, surrounded by photographs and other mementoes of her family and friends, she planned her forthcoming social engagements, wrote letters and attended to the affairs of the household, and otherwise occupied herself with a variety of activities to make the hours pass pleasantly.

The morning room should be 'cheerful and sunshiny, and wear a domestic, cosy look', it was declared in Lady Colin Campbell's *Etiquette of Good Society*. 'It is not fitted up with any particular style of furniture. The curtains and covers will be some kind of small-patterned chintz or cretonne, with a carpet to match. Nothing very grand or very new should find its way into this apartment – nothing stiff or formal. Tables here and there, and chairs of different sorts and sizes, a stand with plants, a small piano, a low bookcase – these are the principal features in a room of this description, a general tidy *déshabille* pervading the whole.'

Ebonized Early English Tables.

The Persian Divan Easy Chair.

The Morning Room

This diary for 1895 was a promotional gift from the Scottish Widows' Fund.

Writing Letters

My dear Annie!

"A merry Christmas and a happy New Year" in the common way are inseparable from each other; yet this forthcoming New year does not make its appearance as a happy one, considering the state of health of dear Adolphus, besides some other rather vexatious things, not to be mentioned here, — and yet we will

Sir Rowland Hill's notion of a postal system, based on the purchase of an adhesive stamp costing one penny, was introduced two years after Queen Victoria ascended the throne. It ushered in an age of letter-writing: as well as letters, Christmas cards, Easter cards, postcards and valentines were written and sent. As the Rev. T. Cooke stated in *The Universal Letter Writer or The New Art of Polite and Commercial Correspondence*, 'Letters are the life of trade, the fuel of love, the pleasure of friendship, the food of the politician and the entertainment of the curious.' The worthy Reverend gave copious advice on every form of letter from 'urgent demand for payment' to cards of compliment and

BELOW: A postcard holder made from carved wood, illustrated in The Lady's Bazaar and Fancy-Fair Book.

petitions 'suited to all the various circumstances of human life'.

The elaborate etiquette of letter-writing was made abundantly clear to readers of *The Young Ladies' Treasure Book*. It instructed that 'No young girl ought ever to engage in correspondence with a gentleman who is neither a relative nor her betrothed, and as a rule, cannot do so without eventually lessening herself in his eyes. With some men it is even dangerous for a lady to write a note on the commonest subject. He may show the superscription, or the signature to his idle friends, and make insinuations much to her disadvantage.'

Elegance and perspicuity were urged in penning even the briefest note: 'Miss Sprightly's respectful compliments to Lady Russell, entreats the honour of her company this afternoon for tea.'

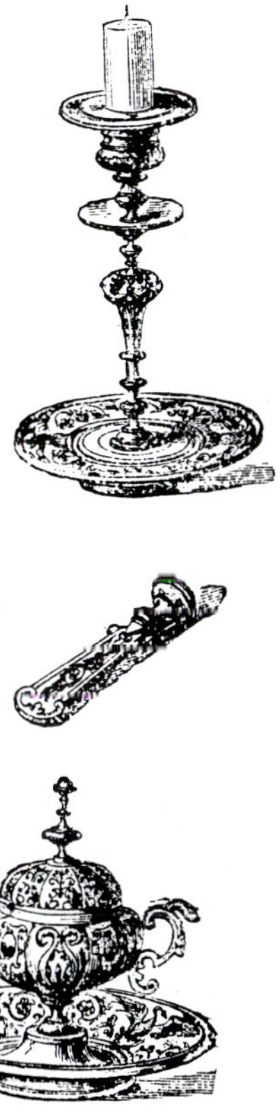

SWEEPING
&
DUSTING

FLOOR POLISHING BRUSHES.
With Wrought Iron Socket.
Best Stiff Grey Bristle, Complete with Ash Handle.
The "County," ... 26/6 each.

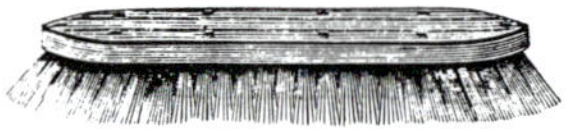

MILK CAN BRUSHES.
The "New."

DUST
Positively Removed.

You know how utterly impossible it is to remove all dust, which daily invades the home, by the use of brooms and brushes. Despite the most scrupulous and ceaseless toil, particles of dust remain lodged in the texture and fibre of articles, thus harbouring disease-germs and being a perpetual menace to family health. The **"Little Giant" Dust Extractor** does what brooms and brushes and human energy can never achieve. It draws out and devours every lurking particle of dust, leaving the surface over which it has passed absolutely free from dust. A brush or broom collects but a small portion of the dust which it dislodges and disturbs, the bulk of the fine dust floating in the air to be inhaled into the lungs or to settle again.

The **"Little Giant"** Dust Extractor does not miss the very finest particles, but draws it all in.

Write for Booklet.

THE "LITTLE GIANT" (Showing Extractor in operation) Cleaning under Furniture.

ROOMS
Free from Dust.

Hitherto a "dustless" home has only existed in the dreams and aspirations of reformers. Now i is a practical and accomplished fact wherever th **"Little Giant" Dust Extractor** is introduce Considering the increased comfort and beauty the home which is assured and the marvellous w it removes risks from infection by disease ger the **"Little Giant"** is a gilt edged investm

REMEMBER!—The small initial outl is the ONLY outlay.

It will last indefinitely.

It will save its cost in brooms brushes over and over again.

Every consideration of thrift, pruden family happiness combine in urging the of this wonderful machine as an indisp feature of the modern home.

Write for Booklet.

"Little Giant"
DUST EXTRACTOR

POINTS OF INTEREST.

It is the most simple and effective Dust Eliminator that has ever been invented.

It can be used anywhere, everywhere, and at any time, as wherever dust can penetrate, the **"Little Giant"** can remove it.

It is simple and easy to manipulate, any maid or even a child can keep a home clean by its use.

Considering its enormous benefits the price is quite nominal, and once bought, "expense" becomes a thing of the past.

Can be seen and purchased at all reputable Ironmongers, House Furnishers, &c., when practical demonstrations will gladly be given.

Illustrated descriptive Booklet free on application to
Sole Manufacturers and Selling Agents:
W. M. STILL & SONS LTD.
24 CHARLES STREET,
LONDON, E.C.

THE "LITTLE GIANT" Easy to Carry. Light and Portable.

REDIO PATENT SELF-CONTAINED METAL CLEANING & POLISHING CLOTH. NO PASTE OR LIQUID REQUIRED.

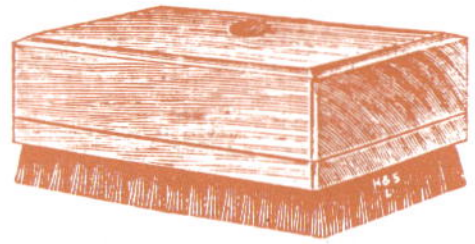

FLOOR POLISHING BRUSHES.
The "London." Best Grey Bristle.
Ordinary ... each 10 6.
Loaded with Lead, ,, 14 -

REGULAR cleaning of the house, from attic to basement, was one of the principal household chores. 'The bedrooms must be thoroughly swept, each once a week. The drawing-room twice a week; but the little pieces of flue and dust should be swept up every day with the short brush and dustpan', directed *Warne's Model Cookery*. Damp tea-leaves were sprinkled on to the carpet and then removed, carrying the dust with them, by vigorous brushing with a stiff whisk.

'When the room is to be thoroughly swept, covers should be thrown over the sofas, ottomans, &c., and the window-curtains should be carefully raised and pinned up till the sweeping is finished, then they should be well shaken out again. Highly-glazed chintz curtains may be kept clean for years, if they are occasionally taken down and wiped over with a clean duster.'

The Young Ladies' Treasure Book reminded readers that 'It is usual for ladies to dust their old china and other valuable ornaments themselves, except in cases where the servant may be trusted to perform this task with unusual care. A servant's fingers are not so sensitive to the sense of touch as those of a lady who does no rough work.'

Florence Nightingale was exceedingly scornful of the general method of dusting rooms, which, she declared, was nothing more than 'flapping the dust from one part of a room on to another'.

KNEELING PADS.

Carpet Covered ... ... each -/10

SWEEPING & DUSTING

ZOKKO.

Specially recommended for cleaning the inside of Baths, Brass, Copper, Steel or Tin Goods.

Will remove Grease or Stains from Carpets, R... &c., and makes an excellent Paint Cleaner. or ...ser for Dogs, Horses, &c.

...6d 1/- 3/6 size Tins.
...5, -/8, 2/- each.

Paints & Decoration

PAINTERS JAMB DUSTERS.

When choosing the paint colour for a room, Mrs Haweis, a nineteenth-century arbiter of taste, thought it essential to consider how the colour might affect the appearance of the inhabitants. Pale, glossy or white papers she regarded as 'ruination to any complexion'. It was important to consider, too, the violent effect of gas light on colours. Although a dark crimson flock paper created a fine effect, it absorbed so much light that no amount of candles, lamps or gas jets could penetrate the gloom engendered by it. It was felt that doors should never stand out in glaring contrast to walls, and as an example Mrs Haweis cited a room with a deep blue ceiling, Vandyck brown walls and deep sage green doors. A red room with a black ceiling

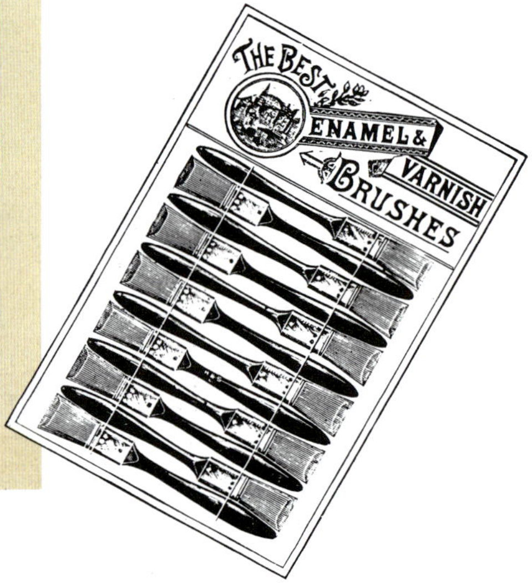

starred with dull sea-green or yellow she thought very bright and good.

With the advent of good proprietary paints many housewives undertook small decorative schemes themselves. Aspinall's Enamel was recommended, testimonials from titled ladies crowding onto its brochure. 'Lady Buxton says: "I have used it in several different colours for wooden furniture, tin cans, glass and china ornaments, with equal success."'

Hobbies & Pastimes

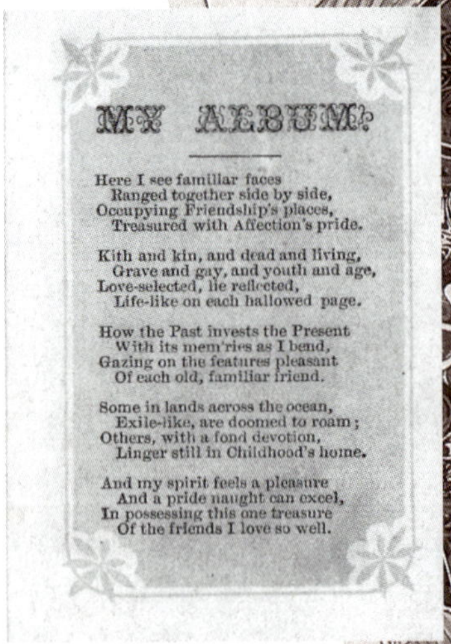

MY ALBUM.

Here I see familiar faces
  Ranged together side by side,
Occupying Friendship's places,
  Treasured with Affection's pride.

Kith and kin, and dead and living,
  Grave and gay, and youth and age,
Love-selected, lie reflected,
  Life-like on each hallowed page.

How the Past invests the Present
  With its mem'ries as I bend,
Gazing on the features pleasant
  Of each old, familiar friend.

Some in lands across the ocean,
  Exile-like, are doomed to roam;
Others, with a fond devotion,
  Linger still in Childhood's home.

And my spirit feels a pleasure
  And a pride naught can excel,
In possessing this one treasure
  Of the friends I love so well.

Hobbies & Pastimes

The practised hostess would see that the reception rooms were furnished with 'albums, illustrated books, photographs, and objects of rarity and interest generally, which are scattered about on tables for inspection', it was said in *Dinner Table Etiquette*. For ladies, the creation of such albums and articles for display provided agreeable entertainment, exercising usefully both the head and the hands.

Making collections of various kinds was an amusing occupation. Besides wild flowers and ferns, dried between sheets of blotting-paper and placed in a book or journal, there were fashions for collecting stamps, autographs, crests and monograms, and photographs of eminent persons, adding to these appropriate quotations. *The Young Lady's Book* suggested designing the page of an album with a fan and incorporating a vignette in each of the leaves. The hand colouring of photographic portraits was another delightful recreation, an artistic exercise that completed 'the resemblance to Nature'.

Mosaicon was the name given to the art of inlaying coloured papers in a framework of wood or other material. This form of decoration was suited to the smallest brooch or miniature frame, or to a large folding screen. Empty cigar boxes provided a useful foundation.

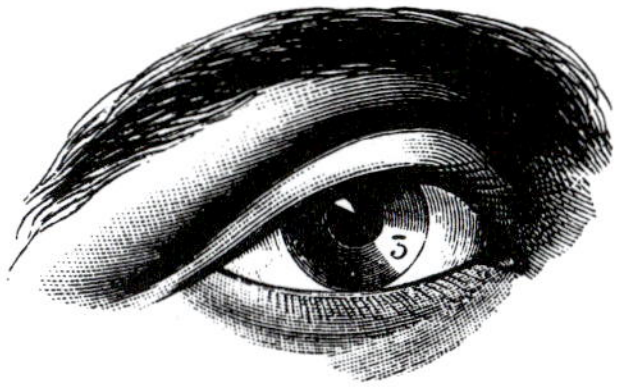

Fig. 8.

Fig. 1.

Fig. 2.

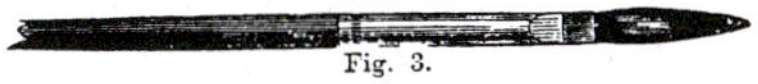

Fig. 3.

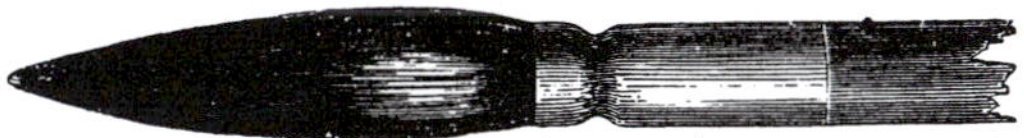

Fig. 4.

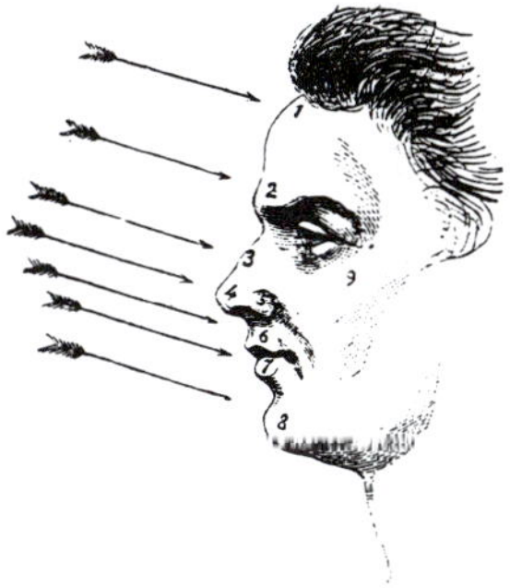

Fig. 5.

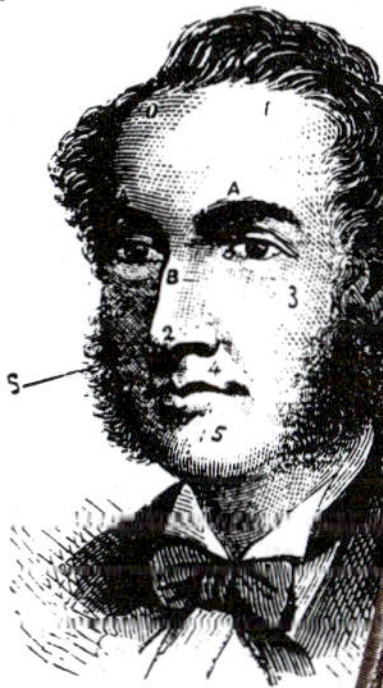

Fig. 6.

PHOTOGRAPHS

KNITTING & STITCHING

OF ALL THE occupations, none seemed so essentially feminine as needlework, it was claimed in *The Young Lady's Book*. The types of decorative needlework that were to be recommended to its readers were point lace, used as a trimming, appliqué work, netting, beadwork and embroidery in

RIGHT: A Labour of Love, *a painting by William Hay.*

BELOW: A *lady photographed at her Berlin woolwork.*

wool, silk or feathers. As to knitting, 'Little girls can knit shoes and under-shirts for their baby brothers and sisters; young ladies can knit socks, stockings, and waistcoats for their elder brothers and friends; stockings and couvre-pieds for their mamma; purses and all kinds of warm things for their papa; and a variety of comforts for the invalid.'

Knitted articles were much sought after at the bazaars organized in support of charitable institutions. A bazaar 'affords opportunities to many idle people of pleasantly exerting themselves, discovers and brings forward obscure talents, promotes intercourse and amusements, and frequently ensures most advantageous returns.' *Beeton's Ladies' Bazaar and Fancy-Fair Book* advised on how to prepare any number of useful items and novelties: cases for powder puffs, tea cosies, foot warmers, needle-books, even a basket for a bathing dress.

It was made clear in *Social Etiquette* that, 'If a lady is engaged with her needle when a visitor arrives, she ought to discontinue her work, unless requested to do otherwise. We cannot avoid hinting to our lady-readers, that even when a particular friend is present for a short time, it is somewhat inconsistent with etiquette to keep their eyes fixed on a crochet or knitting-book, apparently engaged in counting stitches, or unfolding the intricacies of a pattern.'

ENGAGING SERVANTS

THERE WERE various ways of procuring domestic servants. Some mistresses enquired among their friends until they heard of a maid who had given satisfaction; others applied to a registry office such as Miss Kerr's in Lower Belgrave Street and yet other potential employers placed or replied to an advertisement in a newspaper or magazine.

With regard to references from former employers, Mrs Haweis advised that 'No character under one year should be accepted, save under very exceptional circumstances, as it is easy for a woman or man to be honest and steady during a month or two in

BELOW and BELOW LEFT: Photographs of servants to be sent as postcards, perhaps home to their families.

1 JAN., 1891

THE LADY

26

Gig, high wheels, suitable for horse 15 or 15·2; complete, with pair large plated lamps, cloth cushions, rubber mat, leather dashboard and wheel splashes; good condition. Cost when new £50. Photo sent. Also harness, suit cob. Sell gig complete and harness £20. Bargain. No room. 9235

Gold sequins, 2s. 6d. gross; smaller, 1s. 6d.; silver, 2s. 6d. Stars (dress), 1s. 6d. Crazy patchwork spangles, 1s. gross. Beetleswings, 2s. hundred. Sample packet, 4d. 9238

Fancy-dress stars, gold, silver, colours, 1s., 1s. 6d., 2s. gross; sample dozen 3d. 9238

Skates, 9 inches; exchange for 8½ inches, or sell for 3s. 6d. 9239

Side saddle; good condition; comfortable; medium size; £3. 9240

For sale, an almost new parrot's square cage; 19 in. high, by 14 in. wide; has only been used one week. Paid £1 for it; ask only 15s. 9241

Lady's skates; perfect condition; 5s. 6d. 9242

Hand sewing-machine, working order, 3s. 6d. 9242

Bezer skates, 10½; as new. Cost 10s. 6d.; 5s.—9243

Pot-pourri of cabbage and moss roses, 1s. 9d. per 9244

... bags, lined contrasting ... most artistic

LADY recommends her LADY HOUSEKEEPER. Six years. Kind, domesticated. Total abstainer. Church.—"Phoebe," Suppen's Library, Church Road, Brighton.

LADY can recommend lady as USEFUL COMPANION, SECRETARY, READER. Daily or resident.—"A. S.," 2, Stanley Terrace, Norbiton, Kingston-on-Thames.

CAN any lady recommend a thoroughly good GENERAL SERVANT? Trustworthy, good plain cook, and clean; nurse and girl kept; boy.—Write all particulars, stating wages, to Windcliff, Hatfield Road, St. Albans.

CAN any lady recommend good GENERAL SERVANT, about twenty, willing to improve in cooking? Housemaid kept.—Mrs. Humphrey, Pershore.

CAN lady recommend experienced, conscientious, and methodical GENERAL SERVANT? Age thirty; house and family small; good wages.—First application, with full particulars, address Mrs. Gordon, 2, Sussex Villas, Kensington.

CAN any lady recommend thoroughly respectable, trustworthy woman, about forty, as GENERAL SERVANT or WORKING HOUSEKEEPER to a lady in business in London? Plain cooking required; comfortable home.—Madame Aline, 26, Great Castle Street, ... London, W.

... a nice strong, healthy ... NURSE? One

CHANGE OF AIR.

THIS column is set apart for the benefit of those seeking change of air and of those private persons who have accommodation to offer. 1. *The Charge* is 6d. for every ten words, or part of ten words, for each insertion. Figures, if undivided, count as five to one word; price counts as one word; compound words count as two. 2. The General Rules for the Private Advertisement columns, lettered A, B, C, and D (for which see page 24), must be strictly observed.

N.B.—Advertisements of hotels, boarding-houses, or of houses to be let, whether furnished or unfurnished, can only be inserted in the separate list at the end of the private advertisements; at a charge of 1s. for every ten words, or part of ten words, for each insertion.

DIEPPE.—Board and residence in a private family. References given and required.—Madame du P., 22, Rue Blainville a7984

CLERGYMAN'S WIDOW receives one or two ladies into her private family; nice square near Notting Hill Gate; hot bath; most comfortable, refined home.—"Clericus," 4, Union Terrace, Notting Hill, London, W 7546

ST. LEONARDS.—Lady offers comfortable home to ladies, gentleman, or married couple. Terms from 1 guinea. Close to sea. Special terms permanency. 7765

... Home offered a young lady with widow. 7830

MATLOCK.—... moderate. ... Apartments required by a ... to be made

HOME required in London by young lady offe... small sum and services.—"D.," Miss Clarke, ... Park Street, Wellington, Salop.

VISITORS to London and permanent residents ... recommended by clery and others to a comfort... boarding-house, in a quiet square, near the Marble A... Terms, per week, from 25s.; per day, from 5s.—... Jackson's Library, Albion Street, Hyde Park, W.—...

LADY GUNNING receives ladies for board and ... dence. A few unfurnished rooms.—Letters ... "Secretary," Addison Residences, Gratton Road, ...

BRIGHTON.—Superior boarding-house, beautif... situated, near sea. Large, airy, well furnish... Bathroom, smoking-room. Late dinner.—Lang... House, 118, Lansdown Place.

SAINT ADRESSE (Le Havre).—Pension de fami... Close to sea and tramway. English referen... Moderate terms; reduction for winter months.—Mada... Cappe, 3, Rue Marie Talbot.

WINCHESTER.—Ladies can be received in a comfo... able boarding-house, in connection with ... Diocesan Home for Training Young Girls, at from 18s... 25s. a-week, the number limited to five.—Apply to ... Lady Superintendent, Connaught House.

BOSCOMBE (Bournemouth).—Comfortable ap... ments. Excellent cooking. South aspec... Clevedon, Walpole Road.

BRIGHTON.—A clergyman's wife takes ladies ... gentlemen for board and residence. Good ho... Close to sea.—"M. G.," Friend's Library, Western R...

... (Campden Hill, near Gardens ... pretty furnished hous... with three

Engaging Servants

the year, and yet be a perfectly discreditable person between-whiles.' Further, a gentleman's character of a female servant was to be distrusted.

Servants were generally hired by the year, subject to a calendar month's notice, and their wages were paid quarterly. Dismissal without notice or compensation was legal for a variety of offences that included wilful disobedience, unlawful absence such as sleeping without leave, immoral conduct, drunkenness, theft, abusiveness and entertaining below stairs at the master's expense and without his permission.

A servant was entitled to leave without notice in the case of 'immoral conduct of the house, insufficient food, desperately comfortless or infested accommodation (after complaint and non-remedy) or personal ill-treatment so that she stood in fear'.

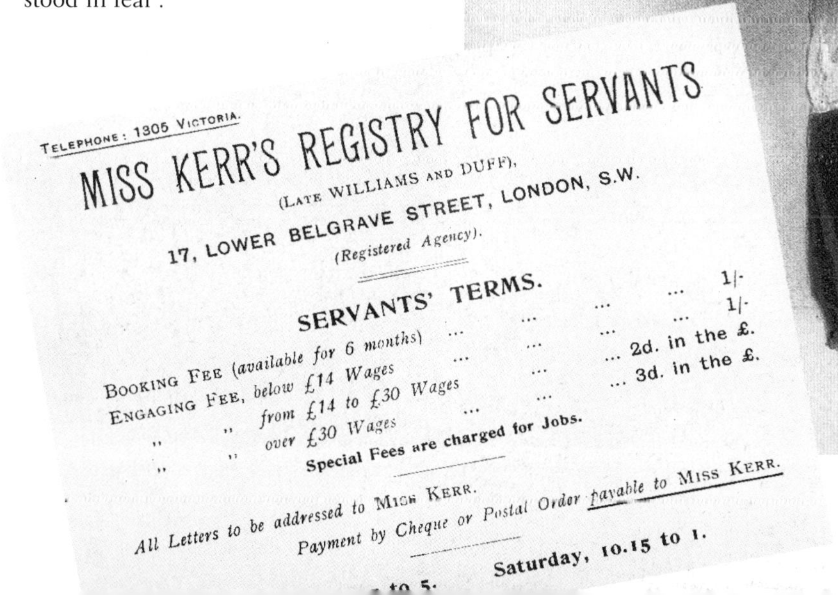

TELEPHONE: 1305 VICTORIA.

MISS KERR'S REGISTRY FOR SERVANTS

(LATE WILLIAMS AND DUFF),

17, LOWER BELGRAVE STREET, LONDON, S.W.

(Registered Agency).

SERVANTS' TERMS.

BOOKING FEE *(available for 6 months)*	... ...	1/-
ENGAGING FEE, *below £14 Wages*	... ...	1/-
" " *from £14 to £30 Wages*	... ...	2d. in the £.
" " *over £30 Wages*	... ...	3d. in the £.

Special Fees are charged for Jobs.

All Letters to be addressed to MISS KERR.

Payment by Cheque or Postal Order payable to MISS KERR.

... to 5. **Saturday, 10.15 to 1.**

Flower Arranging

A victorian maxim for a happy life ran, 'Let beautiful flowers be everywhere, and at all seasons on the mantel of the sick, on the window-sill of the rich, on the tea-table, the breakfast-table and the dinner-table; the very sight of them enlivens, elevates and purifies.' In fact many Victorians were nervous of having flowers in their bedrooms or sick-rooms, believing that their presence deprived the room and its inhabitants of essential oxygen.

Caladium as a Vase-Plant.

Maranta as a Vase-Plant.

Few homes were without pot plants, those with exotic foliage being especially popular; a writer in *The Lady* admired 'coleus in brass pots to be left on sideboard or mantelpiece where they make a point of colour among the plate or china ornament'. Palms, yuccas and cycads defied the depredations of gas and soot, particularly if moved to get the benefit of the morning light from an uncurtained window. Ivy also was robust, and training it around picture frames or in a neat arch around a window was thought to 'render the look-out much more beautiful by softening off the harsh angularities of the builder or architect'.

To preserve cut flowers for as long as possible, the housewife was recommended to put nitrate of soda in the water, and to change it daily. F. W. Burbidge, author of *Domestic Floriculture*, was clear that for the drawing room nothing was more elegant than vase-shaped trumpets of white glass, and gave instructions for the arrangement: 'Do not arrange them in a bouquet, but place a few fern fronds and gracefully drooping grasses in your vase, and these will form an appropriate background for the brighter-coloured blossoms... Floral decorations can scarcely be too light and elegant, a few bold flowers of good form and clear colours being always more effective than a large heterogenous collection jammed together in confused disorder.'

Fountains and jardinières *from a German catalogue.*

The Library

BELOW: A photograph of the library of Wickham Hall in Kent in 1897.

GRAVE AND WARM colouring was appropriate to a library, it was said, which, 'if it is to be a library, and not a mere smoking room, should be situated in some quiet corner, where its occupant can, if desired, be secure from interruption... and not capable of being used as a passage from one room to another.' A north or north-eastern aspect was favoured, certainly not exposed to direct sunlight.

Warne's Model Housekeeper described suitable furnishings: 'The library should have a rich Turkey carpet and the furniture should be of a handsome and stately character of carved oak or rosewood. Above the bookshelves should be busts of distinguished authors. Over the mantelpiece a good picture; on the chimney-piece itself a marble or bronze timepiece and bronze ornaments.' A figure of Hermes (Mercury) was considered particularly appropriate since in the classical pantheon he was the god who was credited with devising the alphabet; alternatively an owl, the attribute of Athene (Minerva), the goddess of learning.

On a more modest scale, for those whose library had to fit into existing rooms, several types of bookcase were recommended. Revolving American bookcases were held to be excellent, taking up little space but holding a great many volumes and allowing for a china figure to be placed on top of them. The correspondent for the *Lady's Pictorial* extolled the usefulness of a plain oak bookshelf that incorporated a central section cur-

tained in velveteen, behind which could be placed 'paper-backed shilling books, that are not in the least bit decorative'.

For the content of the library, young ladies were guided as follows: 'We need scarcely insist upon the reading of the Bible – which in all homes should have first place. Cultivate higher literature first... Romance and fiction should be with you the puddings and sweets of your mental meals. The substantial meat should be enjoyed with good appetite, and the palate merely tickled with romance, which although it has some heroes and heroines, is not of a permanent and lasting nature.'

The Dining Room

A dining room in the Jacobean taste, photographed at the end of the nineteenth century.

Fig. 52.—Dining-room Chandelier.

In the dining room recommended in *Warne's Model Housekeeper*, a refined and elaborate style was favoured. 'The carpet should be rich Turkey or Axminster – not quite covering the floor, but leaving a border of polished oak. The sideboard should be (in the country) of old oak carved, all the furniture matching it; in London of polished mahogany, the cellaret to match. The dining table should be oval, of polished mahogany; the chairs of the same, with leather cushions, harmonizing in colour with the curtains. The side-tables should not be too large; the chimney-ornaments of bronze; on the walls, family portraits, or well-chosen landscapes – not paintings of any painful subject.' The walls should be green but, 'not arsenical green'.

In some dining rooms, Murphy noted, 'the walls have been regarded merely as affording a frame, or setting, to the central table, which, with its decorations, its linen, its glass and its silver, and its environment of guests, partly consisting of ladies in brilliant toilettes, forms the picture. In others, the walls are adorned by objects upon which it is pleasant to look in the intervals between courses.'

Very Superior Library, Smoking, or Dining Room Chair.

The Dining Room

CRUMB TRAYS AND BRUSHES, COMPLETE.
Japanned Blue, with Flowers.
The "Alexandra."
Each 1 8

FIREPLACES & FENDERS

RIGHT: *Fire-irons were described by Muthesius as 'more or less lifeless ornaments', left unused to keep them bright and shining.*

A chimney sweep illustrated on a Christmas card.

As it was stated in the household column of *The Lady* magazine for 14 May 1885, 'There is nothing in the world more suggestive of home-comfort than an English fire. The shabbiest furniture, the most homely surroundings gather new charms in the glow of a bright fire.' The writer disapproved of the old-fashioned rule that led households to refrain from lighting a fire between May and November – or as soon as the spring cleaning was complete. 'A clean-swept hearth and dancing flames delight the heart of the tired home-comer, and no wife should let him return on a wet chilly day to a stove decorated with ferns, or worse still, tissue-paper "because the fireplace is done up for summer".' One correspondent suggested that the expense of coal for a cheery fire in every room and a small stove in the hall was counterbalanced by the saving on doctors' bills.

On the subject of fenders and fire-irons, available in different metals and in a variety of designs, 'To my mind there is one golden rule; brass in the bedrooms and drawing room and copper in the dining-room and library. Popular for the smoking room and not to be despised for the boudoir, are tall fenders about twenty inches high with wide padded seats. These are a great luxury in a "den" where folks are wont to congregate on a cold winter's day, and to clamour for tea and cakes after a freezing drive.'

Fireplaces & Fenders

HEARTH BRUSHES.
Brass Twisted Handle.
Black Hair.
The "Southwark."
Each 1/7

Household Hints

Ivory Knife Handles and other ivory that has become yellow, may be bleached by placing them under a bell-glass in the sun. If the ivory is carved, and the crevices have become discoloured and dirty, wash them with warm water and powdered pumice stone. If very little soiled moisten a piece of flannel with water, dip it in finely-powdered salt, and it will both cleanse and whiten the ivory.

Lemon Wine – Boil two quarts of water with two pounds of loaf sugar until the sugar is dissolved, then add one ounce of citric acid. When cold, stir in with a silver spoon twenty drops of essence of lemon and ten drops of pure spirits of wine. Colour this wine with a few blades of saffron; strain, and bottle.

Have a Duster-Bag in every bedroom, and, in the dining-room, have large squares of cheese-cloth, and keep them in the bags, and in dusting often shake out of doors; when they get soiled rinse them out. These are much better than feather brushes, as the former removes the dirt, the latter merely wipes it up into the air to fall again, being both untidy, and very unhealthy.

When a Picture Begins to Crack after having been painted for some length of time, the trouble usually lies with the medium which was employed in mixing the colours; or sometimes the cause is owing to the painting having been varnished too soon before it had time to become thoroughly dry and hard. The best plan is to consult an artist, who will know, after seeing the painting, how to advise for the best.

How to Revive Leather – Old leather can be made like new by applying a coat of French polish with a camel's hair brush. If the colour is worn off the leather in any places, it is best to colour the polish according to the colour of the leather.

Wine Stains on Linen should be washed out in cold water mixed with a few drops of ammonia and spirits of wine. If, unfortunately, the cloth has been damped before the stains are discovered, wet the stain on each side with yellow soap, and lay on it some thickly made starch. Rub well, and expose to the sun until the stain vanishes. If the linen be laid on the grass and salt substituted for the starch, the stains will disappear in two or three hours.

Flatulence after meals is very disagreeable, and is a symptom, usually, of indigestion, produced, as often as not, by exertion being made too soon after eating. A simple remedy is five drops of pure terebene, taken on a piece of sugar, which is to be allowed to dissolve in the mouth.

Blue Vitriol pulverised and dissolved in boiling water and put into whitewash, gives a beautiful blue tint, and will give a nice appearance to walls badly smoked, or squeeze indigo plentifully through a bag into the water you use, before it is stirred into the whole mixture. Apply as many coats as may seem necessary.

To Waterproof a Felt Hat – Remove the lining, and paint the inside with Canada balsam made hot. Hats made waterproof and not ventilated will bring on premature baldness, so punch a few holes in the side.

Girls who Suffer from Pimples find that watercress is an excellent blood-purifier, and it should be eaten daily with breakfast, it should, however, be very carefully washed before it is eaten. Watercress has a peculiar faculty of absorbing iron from the water in which it grows, and thus, if it is grown on a soil containing much iron, it is excellent for anaemic persons.

Wining & Dining

THE MENU

WITH THE breakfast described by Lady Colin Campbell, various eatables – such as eggs, potted meats and fish – were placed up and down the table, interspersed with racks of dry toast, hot rolls, teacakes, muffins, and small loaves of brown and white bread. The more substantial dishes – such as hams, tongues and pies – were placed on the sideboard. Fish was also on the menu, and kidneys, mushrooms and bacon. *What Shall We Have for Breakfast?* contained receipts for brain fritters, devilled chicken legs and potted ox's feet, among other delicacies.

'Luncheon has been defined as an insult to one's breakfast and an outrage to one's dinner', wrote Lady Colin. In most families it consisted of cold meat, the remains from dinner the previous day. These were to be tastefully arranged: 'A fowl denuded of its wings looks most uncomfortable on a table; whereas, how very different is the effect of its legs crossed one upon the other, and the ungainly ankles ornamented with parsley. The ragged and untidy object is converted into a seemly dish.'

Dinner *à la Russe* came into fashion during the course of the century, the dishes being placed on the sideboard, rather than on the table, and handed round by the parlourmaid. A menu card announced the delights that were to follow.

The Menu

1. Cold Chickens.
2. Lemon Pudding.
3. Potatoes.
4. Scalloped Veal.
5. Salad.
6. Honeycomb.
7. Curried Eggs.
8. Cutlets.
9. Jam Tart.
Menu
WHAT SHALL WE HAVE FOR BREAKFAST?
2nd EDITION
B.H. SMALE.
LONDON
JOHN HOGG - 13 - PATERNOSTER-ROW

WINE & CORDIALS

On the subject of entertaining, Lady Colin Campbell remarked that 'Bad cookery is deleterious, but bad wines are positively poisonous; so if the host's purse will not allow him to give his guests good champagne or hock, or any of the more expensive wines, let him offer only good sherry or claret.'

'Sherry is offered with soup', she wrote. 'With the fish, light wines, such as hock, chablis and sauterne. Champagne accompanies the joint. Port wine never makes its appearance now until dessert, when it divides the honours with sherry, madeira and claret.'

'The peculiarities of claret are now well known', claimed Mrs Beeton. 'Those who have tasted a fine '48 need no other guide as to what is almost "perfect" in wine.'

Health maxim number 1087 in W. W. Hall's *How to Live Long* ran, 'Bear in mind that a drink of water may be more instantly fatal than a drink of brandy.' Hence the bottled water to be found on the sideboard and water filters in the dining room

Idris Royal Table Waters supplied potash and seltzer water, and lemonade, ginger ale and lithia water at between 3/- and 4/6 per doz. 'Water obtained from the company's own artesian wells, over 400 feet deep', claimed the advertisement.

and kitchen. Barley water and mulberry and blackberry syrup were generally home-made cordials; orange and lemon brandy, honey noyau (made with gin), rum shrub, and George IV milk punch (made with rum, nutmeg, green tea, maraschino and madeira) were more invigorating drinks concocted at home.

WINE & CORDIALS

From
J. Schweppe & Co. Limited.
BRISTOL.
4 MAR 1897

We credit you with the following

Returns

Doz.

Half-pint Bottles	@ 2/	
Split	" 1/	
Pint	"	36/
Syphons		6/
Cases		
"		

The Table

The proper arrangement of the dining table was believed to be a branch of the 'household elegancies' of the utmost importance.

To lay the table, 'A white cloth of the finest linen damask is spread *very* exactly on the table,' began Lady Colin Campbell. 'Before each seat is

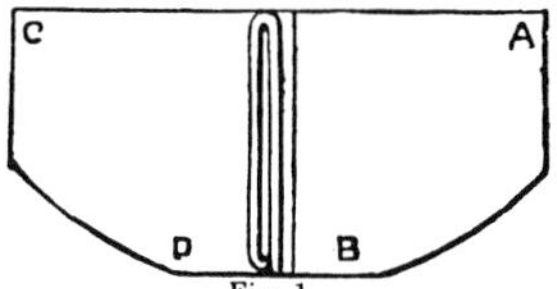

Fig. 1.

Fig. 2.

placed a napkin, folded in some intricate form, and a roll of bread lies within. A knife, fork, and spoon are ready for immediate use, and on the right hand of each person are set a sherry, claret and champagne glass ... There should be a small saltcellar within easy reach of every guest; also a water carafe and glass.'

The manner in which a napkin was folded might serve as a compliment to a guest, according to a Victorian manual. Some specific designs were "“The Boat”, appropriate when a naval chief is the honoured guest; “the Colonne de Triomphe” for the entertainment of a hero fresh from a new victory; “the Victoria Regia” for a distinguished botanist, and “the Fan” for a reigning belle.'

'Willow' pattern was a popular design for dinner services. Charles Eastlake advised against services decorated in pinks, mauves and magentas, hues that were in his opinion 'ignoble and offensive'.

Fig. 3.

TABLE DECORATION

THE 'old-fashioned epergne, which used to grace the centre of the table, has retired into obscurity,' wrote Lady Colin Campbell in 1898, 'and into its place have stepped plants in ornamental pots, and vases of all shapes and sizes filled with cut flowers.' She described a favourite

DISH OF MIXED SUMMER FRUIT.

arrangement of the time in which 'A plateau of plate-glass occupies the centre of the table. On its surface here and there are small china water-fowl or water reptiles holding or supporting bouquets of flowers. The edges of this miniature lake are closely bordered with bright-coloured flowers or green ferns, which are placed in long glass troughs.' This particular design was very effective on a large dining table, she said.

In *Warne's Model Housekeeper* a pretty and ingenious ornament for summer, delightful in its freshness, was described. 'It is a glass stand with a deep bowl-like bottom, surrounded by a rim for flowers. In the bowl, water-lilies are laid; on the second glass-round, which is nearly flat, other plants are placed; on the flat glass top is placed a small block of ice, crowned with, and surrounded by, violets. As the heat of the day melts the ice, it flows down on the flowers on the stands below, and gradually floats the water-lilies.'

The Dinner Party

The carnation and lobster place-cards would have been bought from a stationer.

ONE OF THE first rules of entertaining was that only such persons as might prove mutually agreeable should be invited to a dinner party. 'How often must it be repeated, that it is not good enough to make the most perfect arrangements for receiving company if those invited are hopelessly unsuited to one another? The effect of bringing together an incongruous mass of people is certain and inevitable.'

The 'talking powers' of the guests were to be considered, according to Lady Colin Campbell. 'All the quiet people must not be asked together on

Decanter

one occasion, and all the talkative, noisy people on another. They must be cleverly mingled together, so that they will smoothly amalgamate both as a whole and also one with another when placed side by side round the festive board.' She described 'real talkers' as those 'who have fresh ideas, and plenty of warm words to clothe them in', and recommended that at least one such person was to be secured for a dinner party.

The same expert on etiquette warned against trying to pass off a gardener as butler or footman for the evening, as he was unlikely to possess the necessary dexterity. 'Have we ourselves not felt on one occasion a dish of oysters *à la crème* gliding down the back of our best dress suit?' It was wiser to hire servants for the evening, or plead for the loan of them from a friend.

When dinner was announced, the master offered his arm to the lady first in rank, and he or the mistress of the house would specify who should follow, according to precedence or age. The married guests would take precedence over the single; other rankings included those who were the greatest strangers to the house or those who were likely to be most agreeable to one another.

LEFT: Warne's Etiquette *advised on the carving of all meats from a boiled leg of mutton to a green goose.*

The Billiard Room

A BILLIARD ROOM, to which the gentlemen would repair after dinner for competition and conversation, was an admirable adjunct to a Victorian house.

For the game of billiards an 'ordinary amount of patience and temper' was necessary, according to *The Popular Recreator*. The book contained much useful information on such matters as winning and losing hazards, the cannon and spot-stroke, and the rotary motion of the ball known as 'kissing'.

The rules of the game were frequently to be found affixed to the wall of the room, on a board supplied by the makers of the billiard table. A full-size billiard table measured twelve feet by six, and in the room at least five feet clear all around was essential to allow for the length of the cues. In the age of electricity the lights were suspended from the ceiling and hung low over the table with wide shades.

For houses 'where room cannot be spared entirely for a billiard room' the firm of George Edwards supplied a special billiard and dining table combined. Ladies were evidently more welcome as players on miniature tables and in the less entirely masculine surroundings of the dining room.

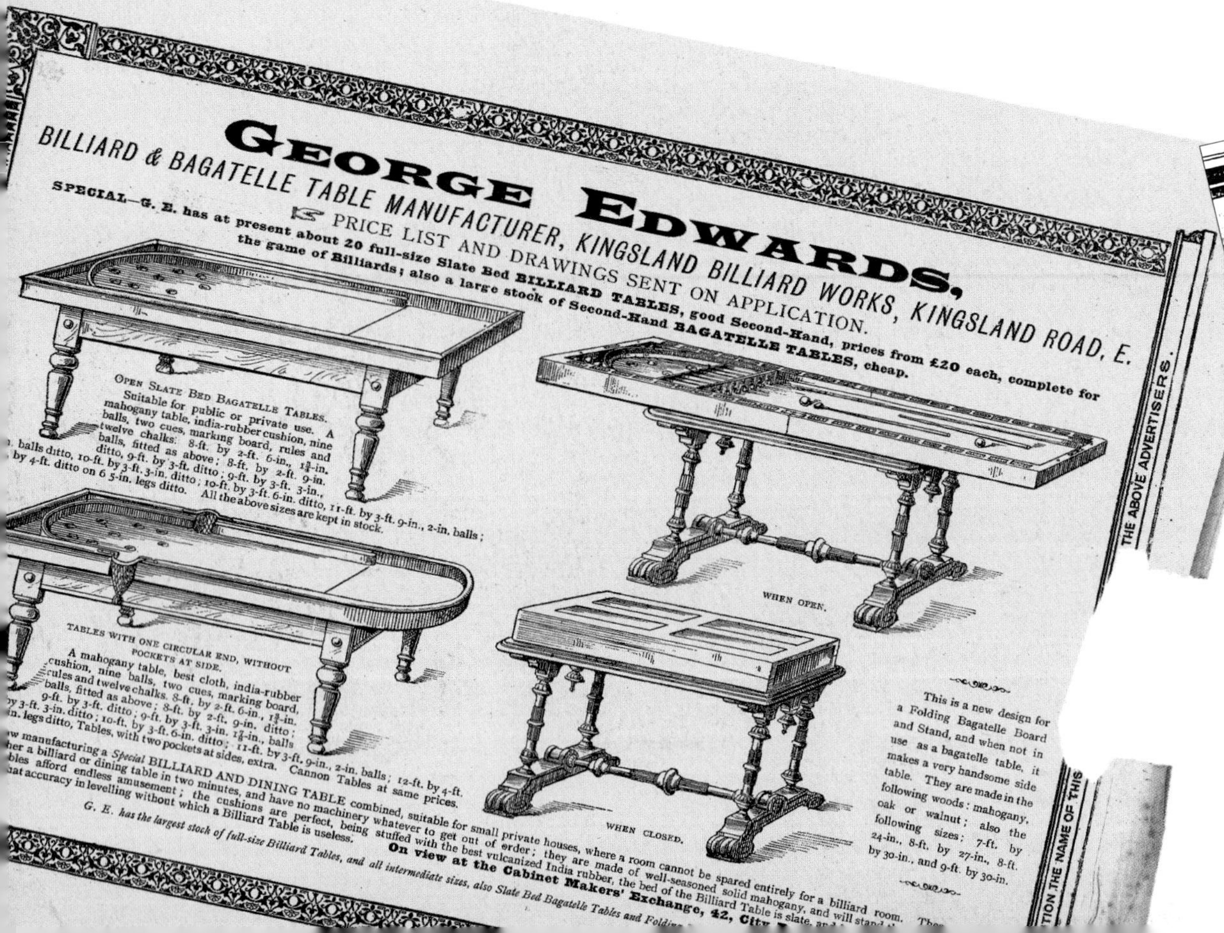

The Billiard Room

Fig. 2.—THE BRIDGE.

THE MINIATURE BILLIARD TABLE.

4 feet 4 inches by 2 feet 4 inches, complete with Balls, Cues, Mace, Rules, Chalks, &c.	£7 0 0
Stand for same.	3 0 0
5 feet by 2 feet 8 inches, ditto	9 15 0
Stand for same	3 7 6
6. ft 3 in. by 3 ft. 3 in., on stand complete	18 10 0

All with slate bed, India-rubber cushions, adjusting legs, and on the most approved models of full sized Tables.

ASSER AND SHERWIN'S
SUPERIOR BAGATELLE BOARDS.

Complete with Balls, Cue, Mace, Bri...

ABOVE: Early electric light used to advantage over a billiard table.

The Smoking Room

DURING THE REIGN of Queen Victoria smoking was acceptable for gentlemen but decidedly *outré* for ladies. As a November 1895 issue of *The Lady* magazine put it, 'these are fin-de-siècle days when every other man you meet has his special brand of cigars and cigarettes and even when, they do say, from the inmost recesses of a fashionable ladies' club, the feminine votaries of the goddess Nicotiana find a secret shrine.'

It was thought desirable for men to retire to a smoking room, especially since tobacco smoke was held to damage fine furnishings. In *The Art of Housekeeping* Mrs Haweis saw the room as one in which 'the tired master should have a place secure from the seamy side of domesticity' and 'sacred from discordant household affairs that are best discussed in kitchen or morning room'. She suggested that it be decorated with his 'books and ancient belongings, photographs of the inscrutable people who were his early friends, gifts from unknown quarters which he still fancies he values.' The wife might contribute an embroidered smoking fez, slippers or tobacco pouch. A Turkish flavour was often considered appropriate for the decoration, and divans, cushions, draperies, pierced brass lamps and a display of Oriental treasures provided an attractive background.

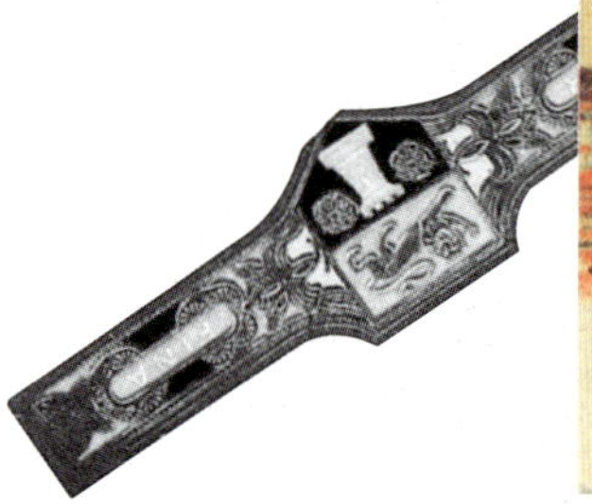

The Smoking Room

LEFT AND CENTRE RIGHT: Gold embossed cigar bands.

50.—CIGAR-STAND AND TRAY.
61

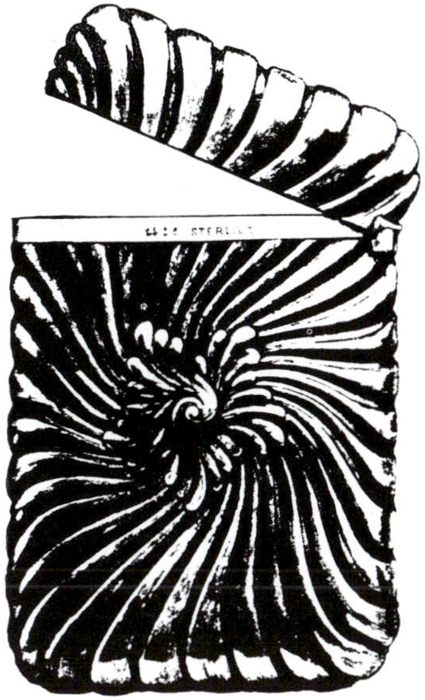

ABOVE RIGHT: A sterling silver match holder from an American manufacturer.

APPLIQUÉ AND EMBROIDERY FOR CIGAR ASH-STAND.

(For full descriptions of both, see letter-press in Magazine.)

Lamps & Lighting

Oil lamps were the principal means of lighting the home during most of the Victorian period. An increased premium was required by insurance offices for premises where paraffin was burned as the lamps were easily overturned, thereby causing a fire. Gas lighting was cheaper, but it was also dirtier.

The variety of oil lamps astonished a contributor to *The Lady* in 1885. 'In less than an hour I saw in Piccadilly and Bond Street at least sixty different designs, and almost as many materials. Bronze, silver,

The Sandringham lamp on an adjustable chain was designed to hang over a dining table.

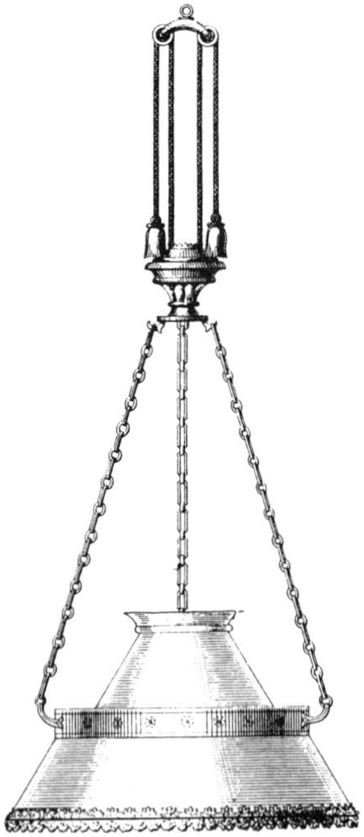

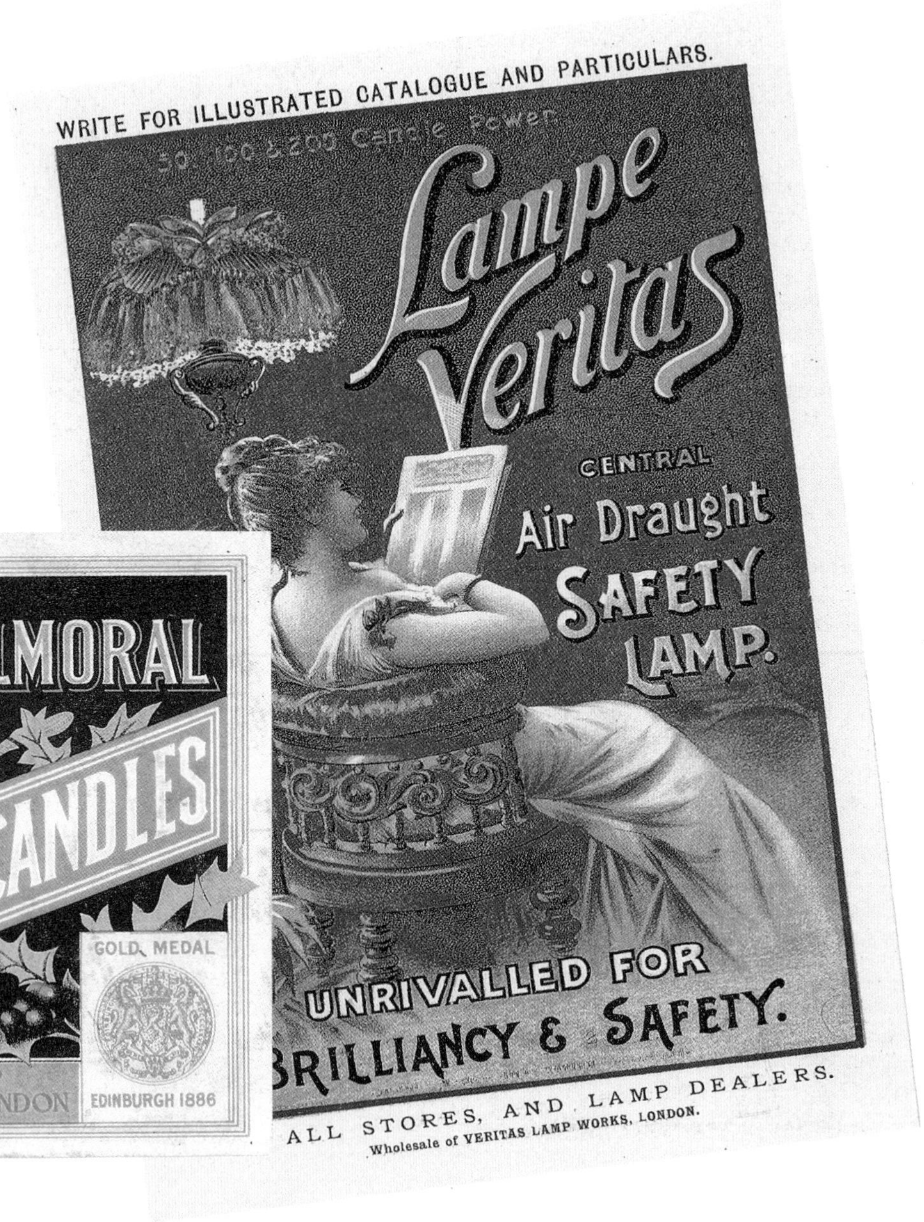

antique and modern china, Japanese and Indian enamels, cloisonné, crackle, gres de Flandres, brass work, glass, even iron work were there. At Williams and Bach's the zoological and ornithological prevailed; here a monkey holds a pendant lamp by rod and chain. . . A rose coloured ibis carries a lamp upon its back, with wings extended and upheld.'

The merits of electric lighting were extolled by Robert Hammond, who wrote, 'Ladies whose endeavour has been, for one hardly likes to say how many thousands of years, to look their best when their husbands or would-be husbands return from their daily toil, will not in future be made pallid by the absorption of this necessary element [oxygen] from the air. They will, indeed, be as fresh and fair in the evening hours as when they are walking along the esplanade at Brighton or taking a canter over the downs.'

I. II. III. IV.

LAMPS & LIGHTING

Household Hints

When Looking Glasses have a smeared appearance, if rubbed with methylated spirit, they will become perfectly bright and clear. The spirit takes all grease away, and dries very quickly.

In Putting on Children's Hoods care should be taken that the ears lie in their natural position, flat, underneath them. If the hood is carelessly put on, the ears may easily be doubled forward by it, and become permanently deformed if the habit is continued. Children's ears are also frequently disfigured by hats which are pressed down too low upon the head, or by the elastics or strings of the hats, which, being carelessly passed under the chin, push the ears forwards and outwards.

To Increase the Growth of Hair in the Eyebrows they may be anointed with a little sweet oil, and the following wash may be frequently used: Sulphate of quinine, 5 grains; alcohol, 1 ounce. This helps to restore the eyebrows when burnt, and may be applied to the roots two or three times a day.

A Mid-day Sleep is desirable in summer for all children under the age of nine, and they should sleep on the bed in a darkened room, with the window open. Draughts should be prevented by a screen placed round the bed, or curtains, for fresh air can do no harm, but draughts, even in summer, are always dangerous. Over-heating and fatigue must be avoided both before and after meals, for those who sit down to table exhausted by heat and exercise run considerable risk of indigestion.

Blankets, after a thorough beating and airing – if they do not need washing – should have sachets of lavender, cloves, and pepper placed between their folds, be wrapped in old linen (keep worn tablecloths and sheets for use in packing), and then slipped into paper bags. Paste the ends of the bag together and lay on a cupboard shelf.

To Make Old Crape Look New – Put a little water in a tea-kettle, and let it boil until there is profuse steam from the spout; then, holding the crape in both hands, pass it to and fro several times through the steam, and it will be clean, and look almost if not quite equal to new crape.

People Who are Fond of Sea-Bathing in summer, will be glad to know that a most effective and yet simple substitute for sea-water is a cup of rock salt dissolved in warm water and added to the bath. A warm salt bath of this kind is the most refreshing tonic for an exhausted body. Do not go out after taking it; just before going to bed is the right time.

Hair Brushes should not be washed in hot water, for it causes the bristles to become soft. Instead, place half a teaspoonful of liquid ammonia in a quart of cold water, and let the bristles of the brush soak in it for a few moments, when all dirt will be removed. Take care that the back of the brush does not become wet.

When the Kitchen is Downstairs the odour of boiling cabbage or onion will sometimes make itself disagreeably prominent all over the house. This can be avoided by putting a few pieces of charcoal into the pot with the vegetables.

Varnish the Soles of Your Boots, and it will render them impervious to damp, and will also make them last longer.

One of the Nicest Contrivances for keeping knives, forks and tablespoons in, is a pocket tacked on the pantry door. Make this of American cloth, and line with red baize, stitching small divisions to fit each article. The baize will absorb all moisture that may be left on these articles.

UPSTAIRS

The Bedroom

'All our Sides, Laths, Stretcher Bars and loose parts are strictly "INTERCHANGE-ABLE" and will fit any of our bedsteads.'

The Bedroom

A foreign visitor to Britain, Hermann Muthesius, explained to his readers that 'In English opinion the bedroom belongs essentially to the woman and it might almost be said that the man merely enters it as her guest.' This he regarded as a 'cultural advance'. One book aimed at new young brides advised remembering that a large part of life was spent in the bedroom, some of it when one was ill and miserable, so it was essential to have 'our bedrooms fresh, pleasant and new'. The author pressed for pretty light cretonnes, mattings, Kidderminster carpets and wallpapers with soothing patterns, 'no turns and twists that shall bother us as we lie in bed'.

Condemnation of wooden bedsteads was general: they were difficult to keep clean and believed to harbour 'certain small animals', and it was thought necessary to burn the bed should anyone with an infectious disease have slept on it. Beds of brass or iron, decorated with brass balls and rails, were universally held to be clean, healthy and cheerful-looking. The lack of draperies was admired as modern, 'not catching the dust or giving the sleeper a headache'. One writer attacked valances as only providing hiding places for boots, boxes, even soiled linen. She also insisted on metal mesh springs and a hair mattress, and allowed an 'unhealthy' feather-bed only under the coldest conditions.

The magazine *Home Notes* ran a long feature entitled 'Daily Care of the Bedroom – This is the most important subject, and one which it behoves the housewife to lay thoroughly to heart.' Proper airing involved opening windows and doors wide daily, putting the mattress close to the window and hanging bedding and night attire for at least half an hour. Maids were told to put on clean aprons to make the beds.

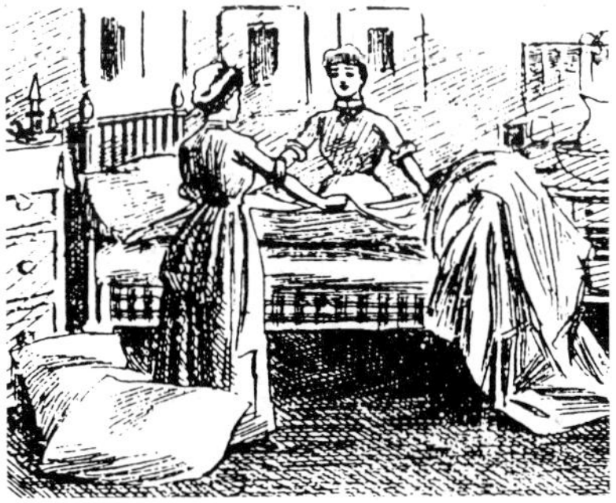

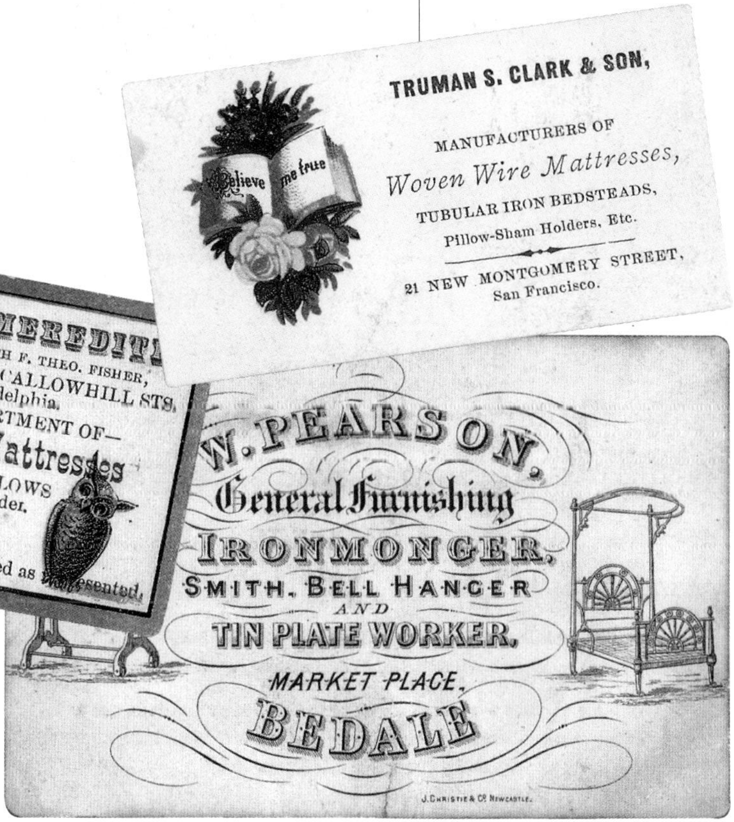

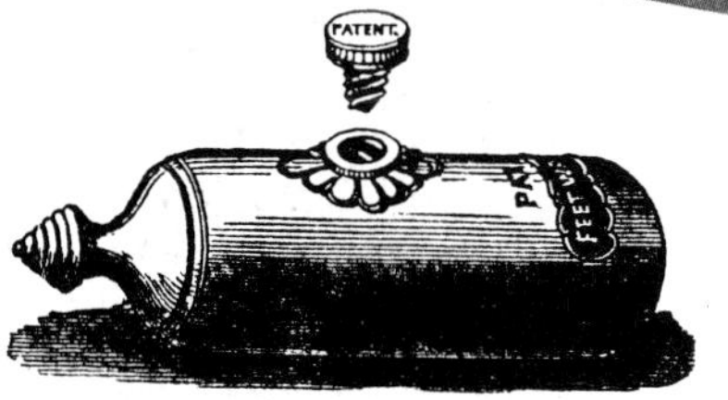

The Dressing Table

In the *Art of Beauty* Mrs Haweis explained that 'Beauty is the natural right of every woman.' She continued: 'The culture of personal beauty, and in our age, especially of female beauty, is of the first interest and importance. A woman's natural quality is to attract and having attracted, to enchain.' She also attempted to console some, 'If you have come to the conclusion late in the day that there are others more beautiful than you, do not give up all attempts to look cheerful and pretty, for after all, you may be for someone yet the most beautiful woman.'

Artifice was permissible, but it must be almost imperceptible. Mrs Haweis avowed that there 'was no more harm and degradation in hiding defects of complexion, or touching the face with pink or white, than in padding the dress, piercing the ears, or replacing a lost tooth'.

Delicate white hands were also considered a mark of beauty, and almond paste was prescribed. It was pointed out that the lady of today was not above 'arranging and assisting such matters as contribute to the beauty of her home', and her hands would be a little less white than if always in repose.

THE DRESSING ROOM

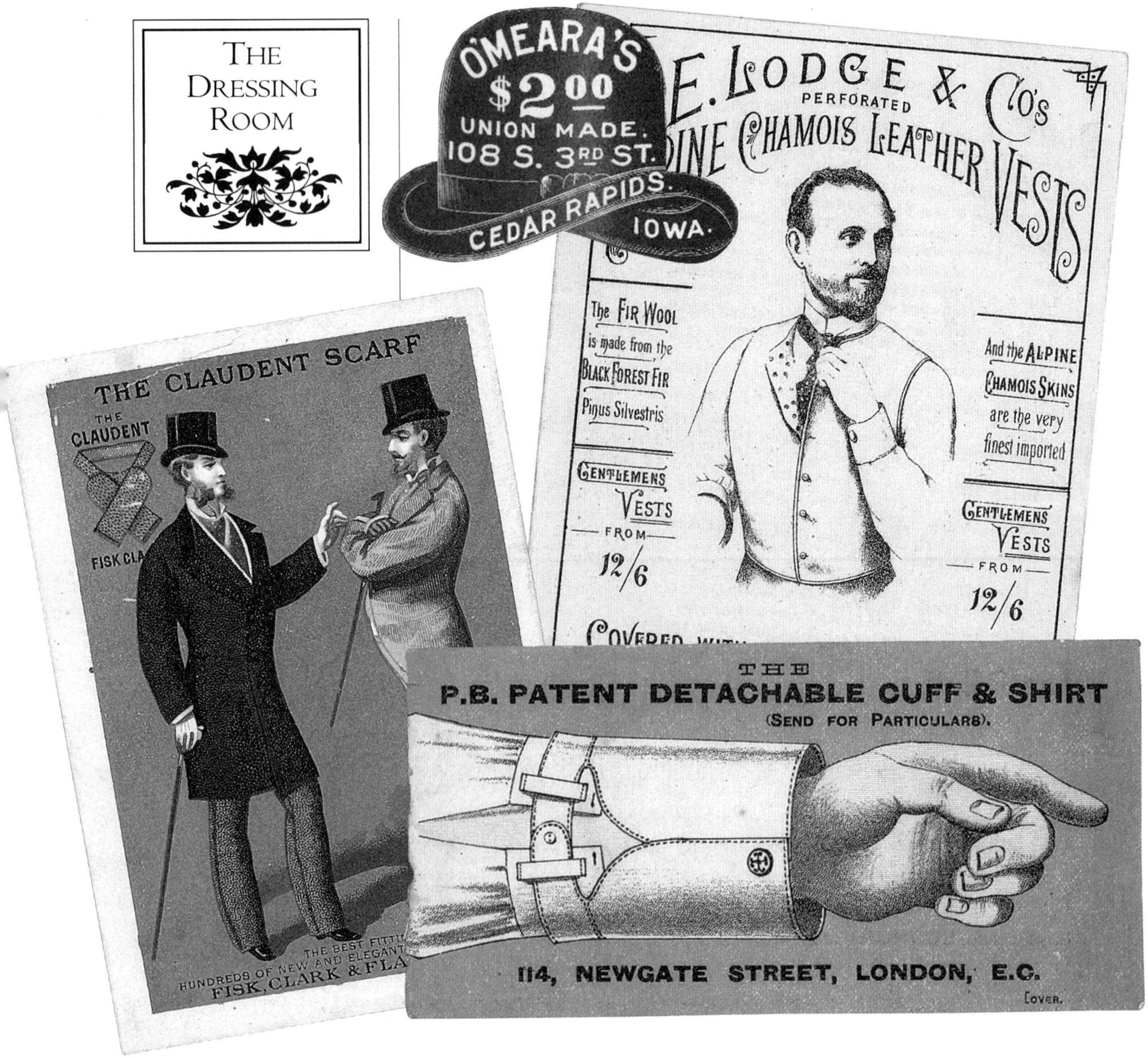

SUCH WAS THE attention demanded by a Victorian gentleman's apparel that one writer declared that it was impossible for him to be turned out respectably without a valet to look after his clothes, and present him with a neatly folded clean umbrella and a decent hat. Mrs Panton, a contributor to the *Lady's Pictorial*, enumerated the essential furniture for a dressing room: a really nice wardrobe, a combination dressing-table and wash-stand and a chair – nothing 'too good' since by their very nature husbands left their brushes out and filled the drawers intended for them with 'sundry bits, scraps of paper, old soiled gloves, spoiled white ties, cartridges, fly-books, bits of gut, string, objects for microscopes and other nastinesses too numerous to mention'.

Harrod's catalogue for 1895 reflected the choice and range of men's clothing which provided the correct sartorial solution for every social, business or sporting engagement. Fifteen types of stiff collar were listed, from the Senator and the St Leger to the Oscar and New Shakespeare. Hosiery and underwear were offered in India gauze, summer wool, white merino, spun silk or tan cashmere. Hats might be for smoking, cricket, tennis, riding, the opera (latest shape with best springs), or travelling (sealskin); a tweed University was for the pocket.

THE TELEION COLLAR.
Keeps any Cravat in proper position. Saves pinning and every other discomfort. "Captain Jaques, Patentee," on each collar. Sold everywhere. Beware of Worthless Imitations.
BETTY BROS & CO. BRISTOL
British and Durable
HYGIENIC HAT ALL COL
NEVER REQUIRES GRINDING
PLEASURE TO USE
REGISTERED
KROPP
REAL GERMAN.
HOLLOW GROUND
RAZOR
Mr. HENRY IRVING writes: "I find your razors excellent."
In Case complete Black Handle, 5/6 Ivory Handle 7/6
From all Dealers, or direct from the English Depôt, Frith Street, Soho Square, London, W.
A. A. FFRENCH'S
BAY RUM
PURIFIED AND RICHLY PERFUMED
ROSE
HAIR OIL,
For Nourishing and Beautifying the Hair.
CARY COCKS & ROPER,
Chemists, &c.
MAN OF ROSS HOUSE,
ROSS.

Home Dressmaking

The invention of the sewing machine by Isaac Merrit Singer in 1851 released women from the tyranny of hand sewing. Thereafter, with the aid of a paper pattern, costing perhaps 6d, or given away free with their weekly magazine, they could create Paris fashions at home.

While much home dressmaking lay in the realm of renovating and updating old dresses 'at small expense', magazine editorials constantly tried to persuade their readers that nothing was beyond their capabilities. 'Shirt-making is quite easy, great care and neatness only being required... I always wonder that Home Dressmakers do not use accordion pleated material more, there is nothing smarter or more fashionable, and yet I have heard so many say it is beyond their power to handle it.'

Many patterns were for the simple and practical: almost indestructible washing frocks for children, an art linen overall useful for gardening, an ideal bathing dress or a carriage wrap. Many mourning wardrobes were also made at home: *The Lady* published careful notes on the depth of crape required on gowns, which 'must be graduated to a nicety, according to the relation in which we stand to the deceased'.

RIGHT: The directions, published in 1854, were for smock-frocks, night jackets, sun bonnets and women's aprons.

HOME DRESSMAKING

THE LADY'S WARDROBE

THE LADY'S WARDROBE

DRESSING WAS DONE by the lady in her bedroom, in front of her cheval glass, 'her faithful friend, which truthfully points out strings and skirts out of place'.

In *The Art of Beauty* Mrs Haweis pronounced that 'Dress is the second self, a dumb self, yet a most eloquent expositor of person.' Writing in 1878, she was part of a movement in favour of a more 'rational' dress. 'If we had but half the flounces and furbelows, we should have just half the difficulty in combining and arranging effects.' The principal villain was the corset; she conceded that people without a corset looked slovenly, but 'we must protest against a machine that, pretending to be a servant, is, in fact, a tyrant – that aspiring to embrace, hugs like a bear.'

Her hints included the suggestion that the stout should wear nothing but black, and that large feet should never be cased in kid, least of all white kid. The thin should never be the least *décollетté* and should put a little padding in their gowns. On colours, she opined that red was inadmissible in close proximity to the face. For the young she approved primrose, which mixed well with plum and maroon and, unlike mustard or chrome yellow, looked well by gas or candle light.

BELOW: *An advertisement for the Ladies' Dress Cap Department of Wadleigh's in Boston.*

The Bath Room

NINETEENTH-CENTURY household books did not stint on the instructions for bathing, since the age had come 'when every new house of forty-five or fifty pounds rental value is considered incomplete without its bath-room'. However, it was acknowledged that even in 1888, when Mrs Panton wrote *From Kitchen to Garret*, 'sometimes even now old houses have not bathrooms'. In this case baths should be taken on a large square of oilcloth, covered by a 'bath blanket'. These might be decorated with feather stitch borders or cross stitch cyphers worked in tapestry wool.

The plumbing expert S.F. Murphy, in his book *Our Homes and How to Make Them Healthy*, expounded the virtues of baths made from copper, rather than zinc, porcelain or concrete, and deemed a shower bath to be without doubt 'an invigorating adjunct'.

No.28.—COMBINATION BATH

Made in either Tinned Iron or Strong Zinc Japanned inside and out.

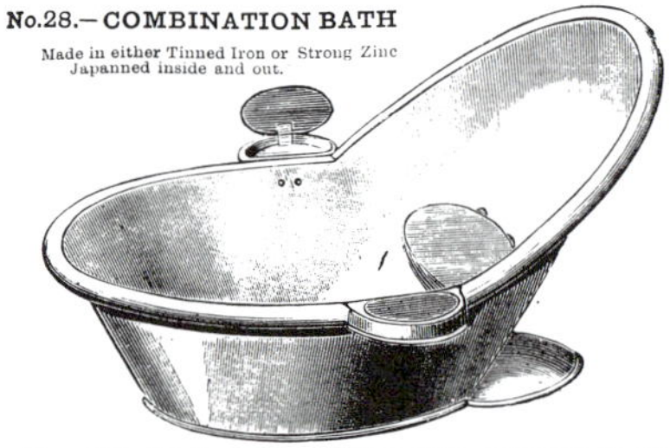

Size outside, 43 inches Strong Zinc, 24/0 Tinned Iron, 28/0
Above combines Hip Bath, Sponge Bath, Sitz Bath, and Child's Plunging Bath.

Whereas warm baths were recommended for cleanliness (care being taken not to remain there too long, an error which would certainly have had a debilitating effect), it was the daily cold bath which was held to be an invaluable aid to promoting health; 'but if the skin turns blue, the practice must be given up.'

The Bath Room

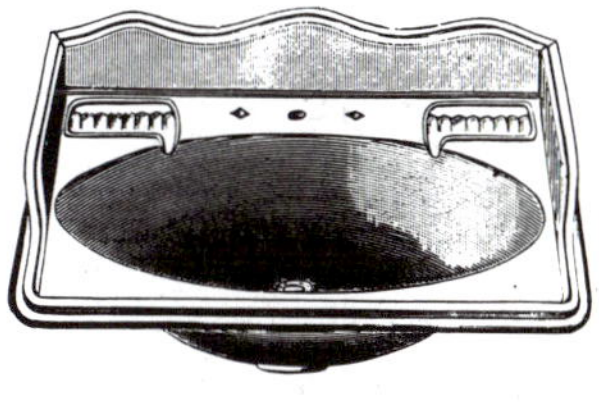

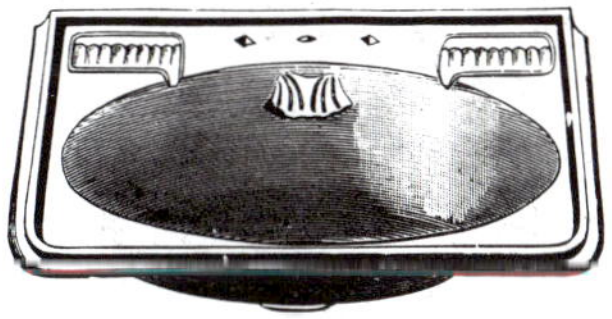

ABOVE: The 'lavatory basin' was available in white, marbled or decorated in colours.

225 —Bathing Slipper.

The Water Closet

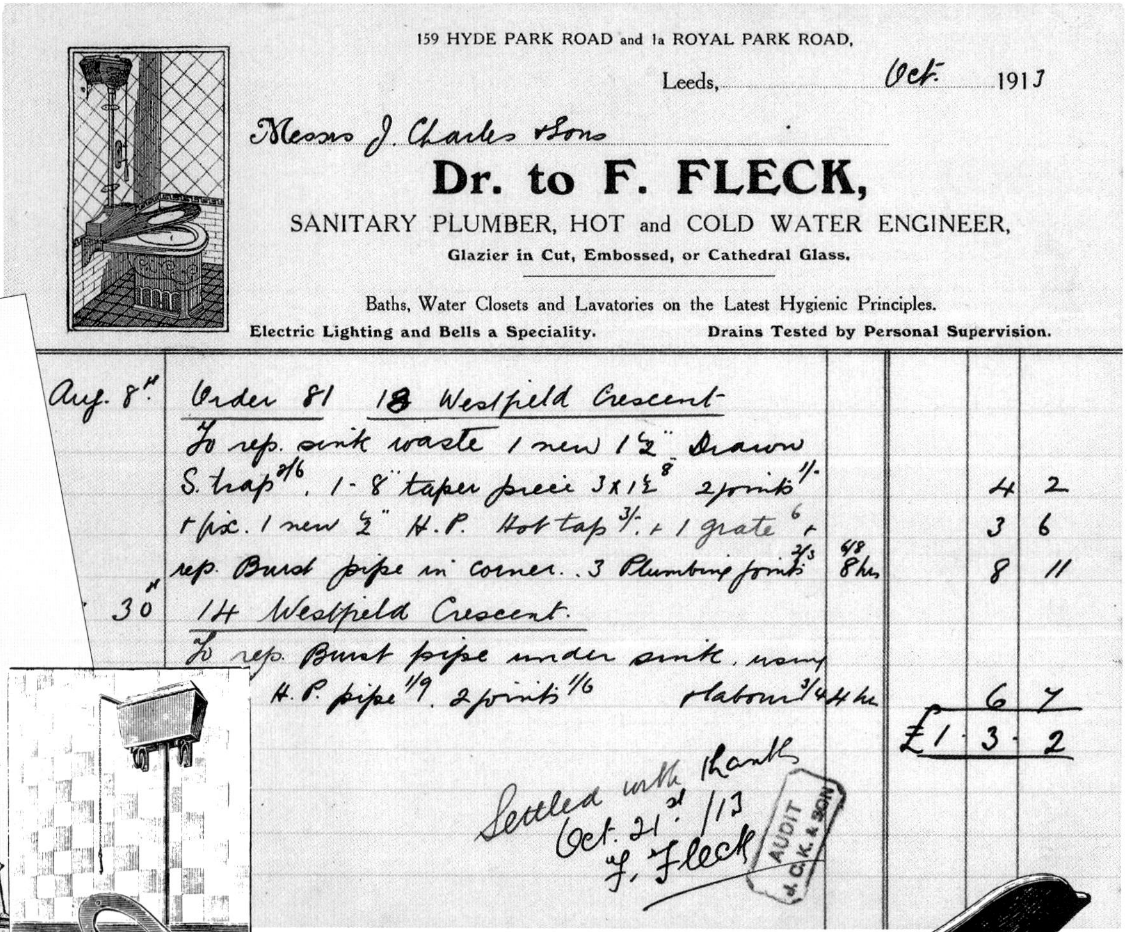

159 HYDE PARK ROAD and 1a ROYAL PARK ROAD,

Leeds, Oct. 1913

Messrs J. Charles & Sons

Dr. to F. FLECK,

SANITARY PLUMBER, HOT and COLD WATER ENGINEER,

Glazier in Cut, Embossed, or Cathedral Glass.

Baths, Water Closets and Lavatories on the Latest Hygienic Principles.

Electric Lighting and Bells a Speciality. **Drains Tested by Personal Supervision.**

Aug. 8th	Order 81 18 Westfield Crescent				
	To rep. sink waste 1 new 1½" Drawn				
	S. trap 2/6. 1-8" taper piece 3x1½ 8 2 joints 1/-			4	2
	& fix. 1 new ½" H.P. Hot tap 3/- & 1 grate 6 &			3	6
	rep. Burst pipe in corner. 3 Plumbing joints 2/3	4/8 8 hrs		8	11
30th	14 Westfield Crescent.				
	To rep. Burst pipe under sink, using				
	H.P. pipe 1/9. 2 joints 1/6 & labour 3/4 4 hrs			6	7
			£1	3	2

Settled with thanks Oct. 21st /13 F. Fleck

AUDIT J. C. K. & SON

No. 32.—SANITARY LAVATORY STANDS.

Registered Design

Fitted with Tiled Back, Bevelled Edge Mirror, and B
For Prices, &c., see next page.

Orders for Cast Iron Lavatory Stands amounting to not less
pages 390 to 403, can be delivered direct from Works, Carriage
to **Liverpool, Manchester, York, Bristol, Birmingham, Edinb**
Dublin and Belfast, or to any other railway station where the
Works does not exceed **30/0 per ton.**

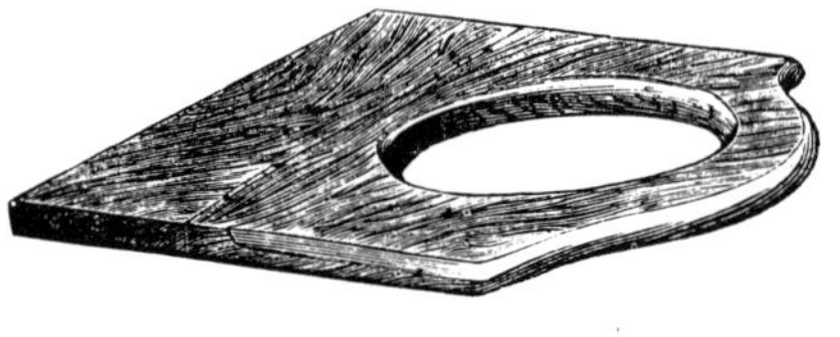

IN 1885 when Arthur Ashwell applied for a patent for his lavatory lock displaying 'Engaged' or 'Vacant' – an Indicating Door-Fastening to a Closet – it reflected the fact that a large proportion of Victorian homes possessed flushing lavatories. These they referred to as water-closets, a lavatory being a plumbed-in hand-basin with taps.

Plumbing and drainage were rather imperfect sciences in the housebuilding trade at that time, and much concern was expressed over the sweetness of the closet. Shirley Foster Murphy was keen to promote 'an ingenious contrivance for mixing a small quantity of some disinfecting fluid with the water in the basin every time the closet is used', but many families made do with pots of scented-leaf geraniums on the window sill.

Ceramic manufacturers competed to offer the finest water closets: George Howson and Co. produced the Condor, Swift and Valkyrie, while The Deluge was made by Twyfords. The porcelain was elaborately decorated with blue dragon, ivy or chrysanthemum designs.

The Water Closet

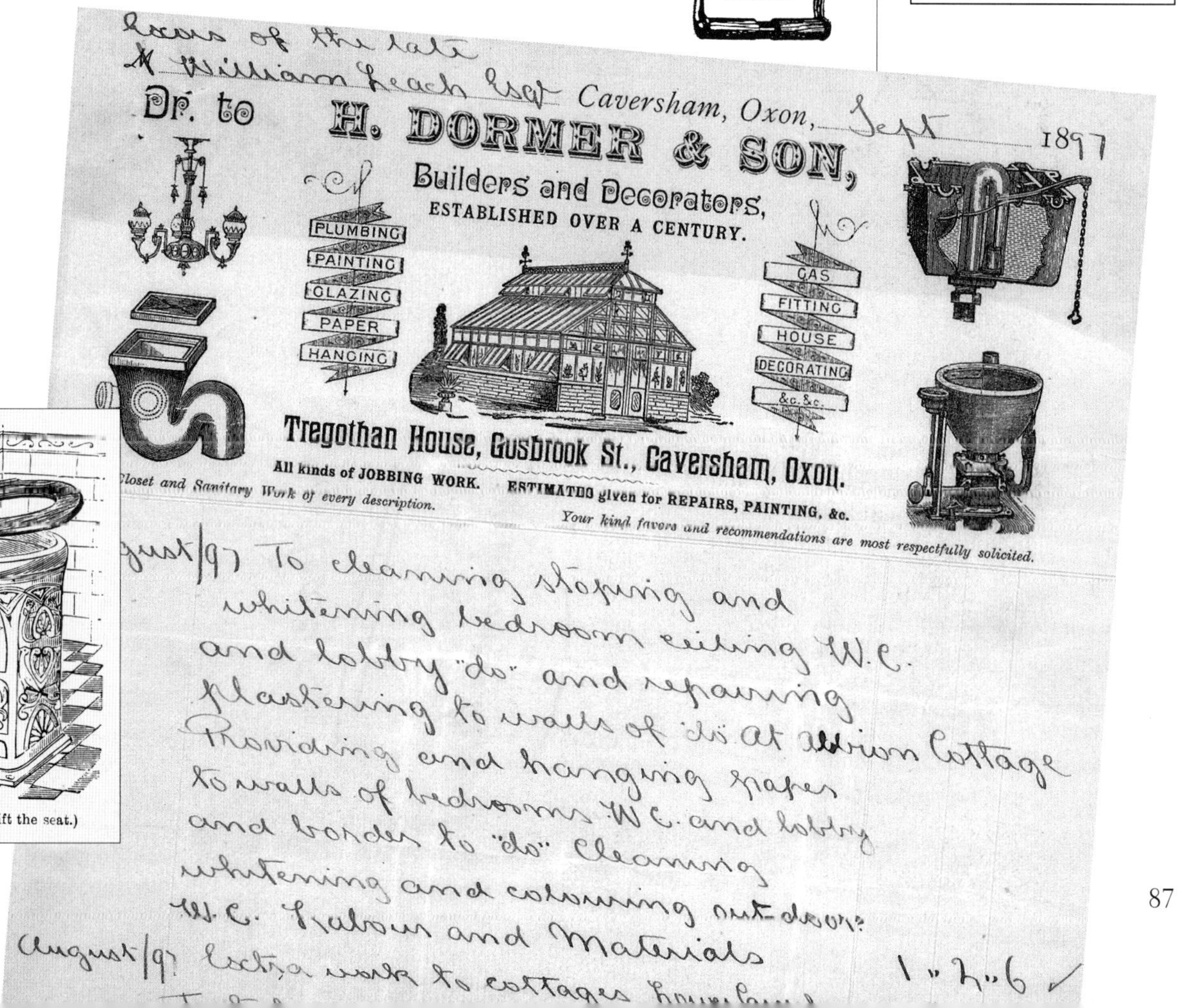
Exors of the late
Mr William Leach Esq
Caversham, Oxon, Sept 1897

Dr. to **H. DORMER & SON,**
Builders and Decorators,
ESTABLISHED OVER A CENTURY.

PLUMBING
PAINTING
GLAZING
PAPER
HANGING

GAS
FITTING
HOUSE
DECORATING
&c. &c.

Tregothan House, Gusbrook St., Caversham, Oxon.
All kinds of JOBBING WORK. ESTIMATES given for REPAIRS, PAINTING, &c.
Closet and Sanitary Work of every description.
Your kind favors and recommendations are most respectfully solicited.

August/97 To cleaning stopping and whitening bedroom ceiling W.C. and lobby "do" and repairing plastering to walls of "do" at Albion Cottage Providing and hanging paper to walls of bedrooms W.C. and lobby and border to "do" Cleaning whitening and colouring out-doors W.C. Labour and Materials

August/97 Extra work to cottages ... 1 " 2 " 6 ✓

W.C. PULL.

Brass Chain with Earthenware "Pull."
1/1 each.
11/0 per doz.

(To use as Urinal or Slop Sink lift the seat.)

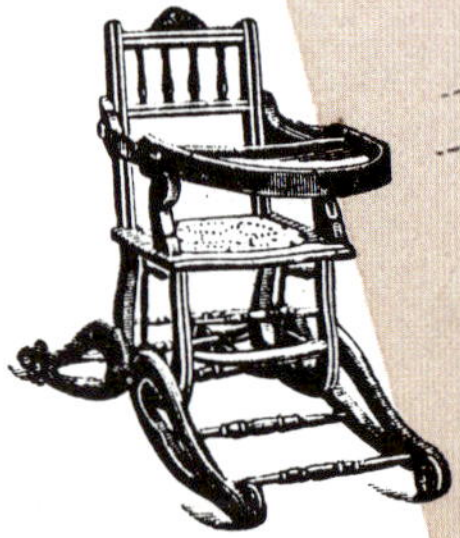

THE CUSTOM in the Victorian household was for children to be hardly seen or heard; Mrs Panton, the author of *From Kitchen to Garret*, deplored the fact that so many nurseries were tucked away in attics, 'far from humanity's reach', in order that the parents might not hear their children's cries or have their china shaken by little feet rushing and jumping overhead. Hermann Muthesius noted similarly how it was possible to visit a house and have no idea that children existed within it. They were under the care of a nurse, who was duty-bound not to leave them for an instant day or night. In many households the children would be brought down to their parents in the drawing room between tea-time and dinner. This regime he declared excellent, resulting in children 'sound of mind and body with stability, toughness and steadfastness of character'.

Mrs Panton described the perfect nursery as containing a sofa. This she regarded as a never-failing inspiration for good games, becoming a fortress, city, iceberg or elephant. Improving pictures for the nursery wall were likewise essential: 'Better to spend your money on showing them good pictures, beautiful scenery and celebrated men, than on aimless gaiety, idiotic balls, smart clothes and expensive food.'

Pills & Potions

To call a doctor was an expense, so the Victorian housewife would keep a small supply of remedies for common ailments, such as camomile flowers, camphorated spirits, castor oil, Epsom salts, hartshorn, jalap powder, senna leaves, sal volatile, salt of wormwood and tincture of myrrh. Anne Cobbett gave receipts for gout cordial and suggested mustard whey for dropsy, garlic syrup for whooping cough, elder ointment for a sprain and almond emulsion for chest tightness.

The author of *How to Live Long; or Health Maxims, Physical, Mental and Moral* wrote that good drains, fresh air, pure water, no corsets and

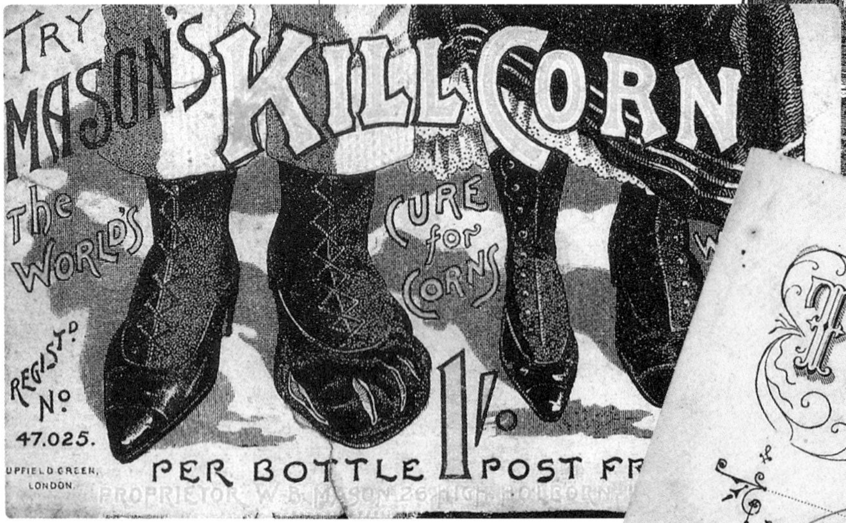

an abstinence from alcohol were the foundations of good health. 'When a simpleton wants to get well he buys something to take, the wise man gets something to do,' he wrote. Proprietary medicines, with unspecified ingredients and miraculous powers, were hugely popular, and the 'simpleton' might choose from the following listed by the Harrod's drug department in 1895: Albert's Grasshopper Ointment, Benger's Peptonised Jelly, Cupiss' Constitutional Balls, Dredge's Heal All, Rooke's Elixir, Oppenheim's Bi-Palatinoids or Count Mattei's Globules.

PILLS & POTIONS

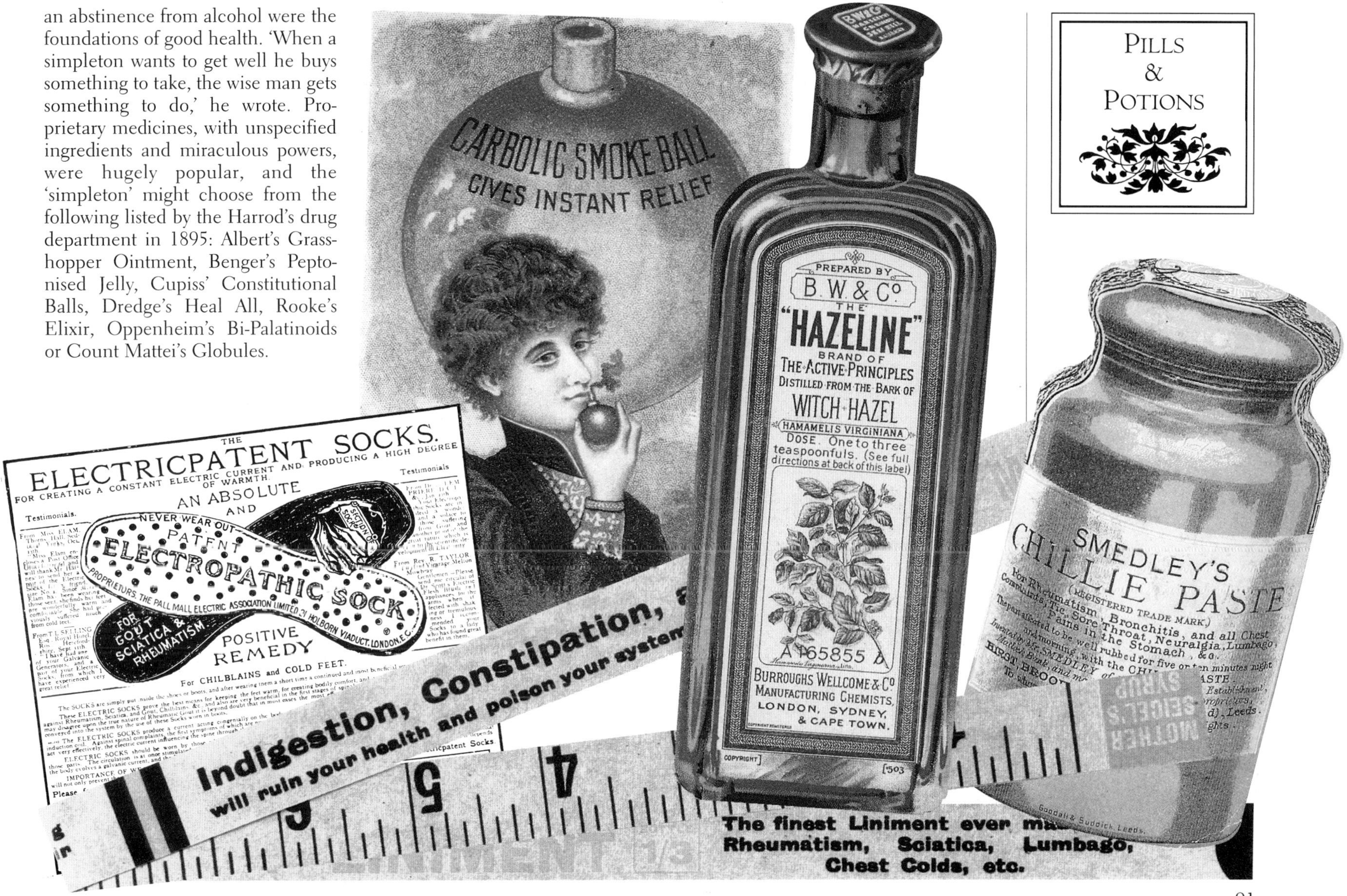

To Restore Scorched Linen – Take two onions, peel and slice them, and extract the juice by squeezing or pounding them. Then cut up half an ounce of white soap, and two ounces of Fuller's earth; mix with them the onion juice and half a pint of vinegar. Boil this composition well, and spread it, when cool, over the scorched part of the linen, leaving it to dry thereon. Afterwards wash out the linen.

How to Prevent Freezing in Cellars – A cellar in which there is no heat can be made warm enough to prevent freezing in it by the use of brown paper or newspapers. Sweep down the walls and ceiling joists to remove the dust. Then cover them with paper four or five layers thick, pasting them over the lower edges of the joists, leaving air spaces between them and the floors above. In covering the side walls it is not necessary to press the paper into the interstices or uneven places.

Tips on Laying Linoleum – While it is difficult to follow a system in fitting oil-cloth and linoleum, a few cardinal rules must be observed.

In cutting linoleum from a diagram, allow an inch at the ends. If it is not to be laid at once allow also a fraction on the width, for shrinkage is probable both ways. Get the diagram correct to the fraction of an inch, so that if cutting must be done for centre pieces or register holes, it can be done before the cloth is laid on the floor.

Smooth the floor by planing the planks. Do not try to make it even by laying strips of paper lining over unevenness in the floor.

Flour, like Butter, Absorbs Odours readily, and should not be kept in a place where there are onions, fish vegetables, or other odorous substances, nor in a damp room or cellar. Keep it in a cool, airy dry room, where it will not be exposed to a freezing temperature, nor to one above 70 degrees. Always sift before using.

Three Recipes for Fly Papers – A very good one, is linseed oil thickened with rosin. Another, three parts of rosin, four parts of rape-seed oil. Or boil to a thick paste, one pound of rosin, three and one half ounces of treacle, and the same of linseed oil.

Rats Can be Driven Out of a House by depriving them of water. They can live almost indefinitely without food, and, when hard pushed, will not hesitate to eat each other, but no rat can go twenty-four hours without drink, and if every possible means of obtaining water is taken from them, they will desert the vicinity.

When Cooking it is convenient to have an iron holder attached by a long string to the waistband, for it saves burnt fingers or scorched aprons, and is always at hand.

The Oil Left from a Box of Sardines is an excellent addition to fish-balls, or any kind of minced fish instead of butter.

Behind the Scenes

The Maid's Room

In *Our Homes and How to Make Them Healthy* it was noted with disapproval that 'The sleeping accommodation provided for servants is too often of a very objectionable character.' The rooms were in the attic or basement, where the lighting and the ventilation were poor. 'Each room, however small, should have a good-sized window, which must be made to open at top and at bottom.'

'Why should not servants have a neat and pretty room? It would be one means of civilizing them and improving their tastes,' commented *Warne's Model Housekeeper*, 'and surely they require baths even more than their mistresses do.' Apart from an iron bedstead and a cheap chair, a hip-bath was recommended, and a bookshelf, a table with an inkstand, a flower vase or two and a good text to brighten the wall.

Fine dresses and aprons, to be provided by the mistress, were advertised as encouraging maids to take pride in their work.

Maple & Co. advertised stout useful Yorkshire blankets for servants.

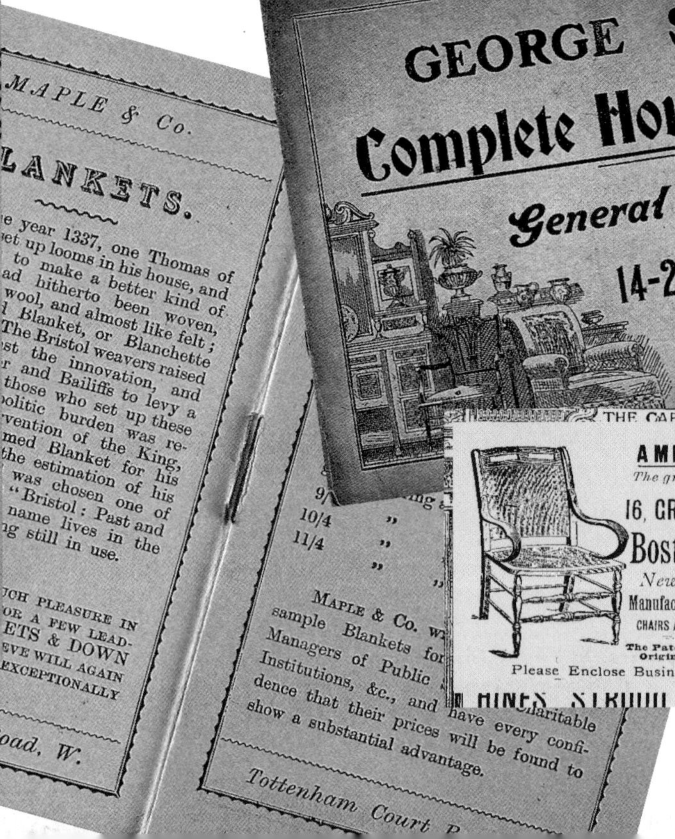

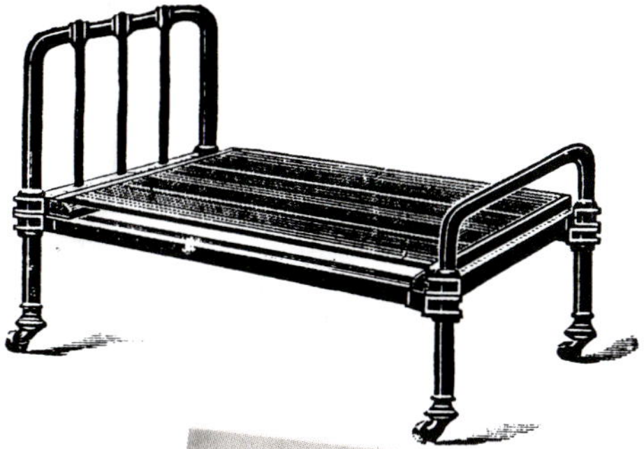

The Maid's Room

LEFT: An improving text from the Bible.

THE SERVANTS' HALL

A CONTENTED household was one where adequate arrangements were made for the comfort and general well-being of the servants. An 'attainable luxury' in larger establishments was a parlour where the servants could eat and rest between duties. The room was generally situated close to the back door for the convenience of answering the bell.

'Besides the indispensable table and chairs, there should be a couple

CALENDERS.

A painting by Charles Hunt entitled High Life Below Stairs.

of armchairs (the ordinary Windsor armchair, with a cushion, is most comfortable, and so is the ordinary hammock chair), and if there is anywhere an old-fashioned sofa still whole, though no longer "drawing-room company", as the children say, this will be an immense boon, especially where there are young maids, who are as disposed to outgrow their strength as any other girls. A few shelves for books, writing desk, &c., is another comfort that costs but little,' wrote S. Beaty-Pownall in her *Household Hints*, 'though adding enormously to the homelike feeling, without which it is well nigh impossible to keep (even supposing one gets) steady, respectable servants.'

Here, in the room in which they took their ease, the servants gathered to discuss the foibles of their mistress and entertain to tea and gossip with the occasional caller.

ELECTRIC BELL PULLS.

THE SERVANTS' HALL

FAR RIGHT: A scale of standard wages was included in Mrs Massey's Servants' Book.

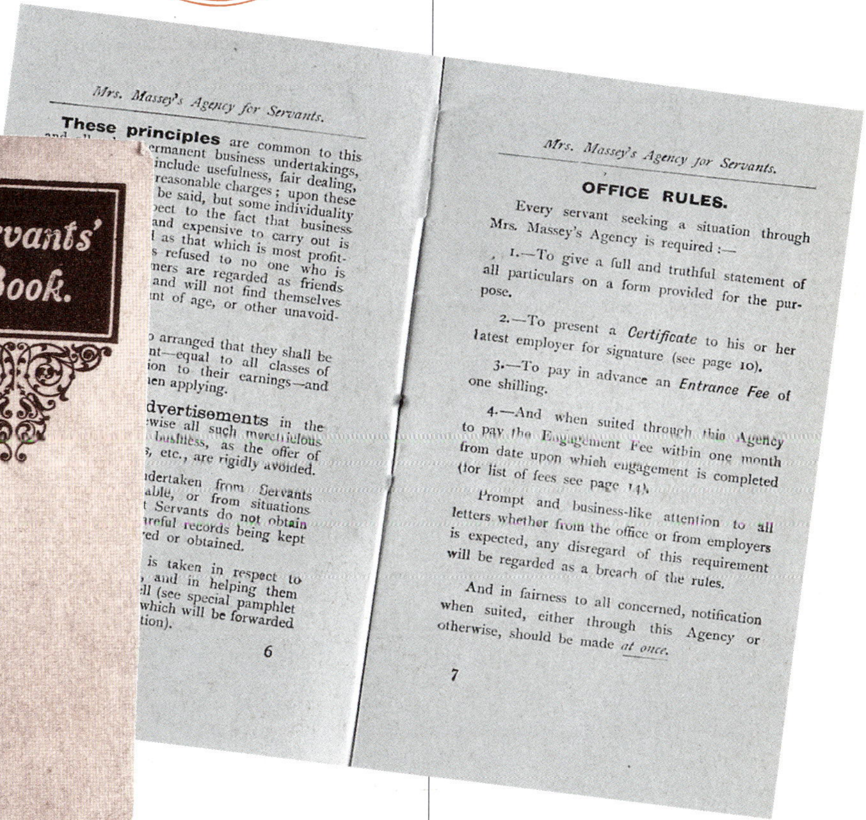

Mrs. Massey's Agency for Servants.

These principles are common to this
ermanent business undertakings,
include usefulness, fair dealing,
reasonable charges; upon these
be said, but some individuality
pect to the fact that business
and expensive to carry out is
l as that which is most profit-
s refused to no one who is
mers are regarded as friends
and will not find themselves
int of age, or other unavoid-

o arranged that they shall be
nt—equal to all classes of
ion to their earnings—and
ien applying.

dvertisements in the
wise all such meretricious
business, as the offer of
s, etc., are rigidly avoided.

ndertaken from Servants
able, or from situations
t Servants do not obtain
areful records being kept
red or obtained.

is taken in respect to
, and in helping them
ll (see special pamphlet
which will be forwarded
tion).

6

Mrs. Massey's Agency for Servants.

OFFICE RULES.

Every servant seeking a situation through Mrs. Massey's Agency is required:—

1.—To give a full and truthful statement of all particulars on a form provided for the purpose.

2.—To present a *Certificate* to his or her latest employer for signature (see page 10).

3.—To pay in advance an *Entrance Fee* of one shilling.

4.—And when suited through this Agency to pay the Engagement Fee within one month from date upon which engagement is completed (for list of fees see page 14).

Prompt and business-like attention to all letters whether from the office or from employers is expected, any disregard of this requirement will be regarded as a breach of the rules.

And in fairness to all concerned, notification when suited, either through this Agency or otherwise, should be made *at once.*

7

THE LAUNDRY

MONDAY WAS washday, and in households where the washing was done at home, rather than sent out, it was regarded by those involved as the worst day of the week. 'Keep your temper on washing-day. Washing is the hardest work women do, but it must be done.'

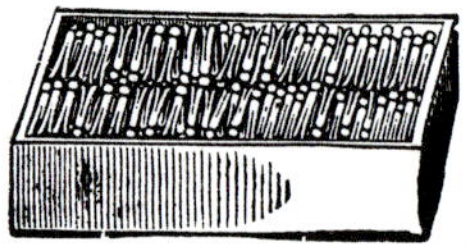

CLOTHES PEGS.

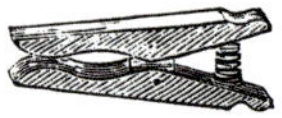

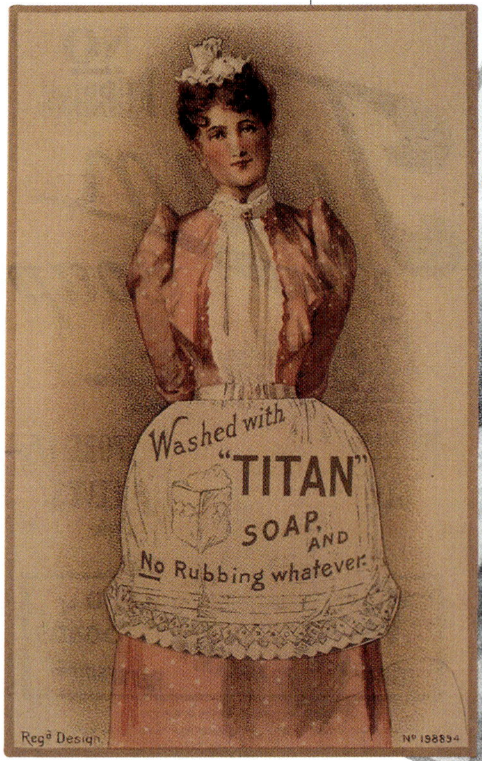

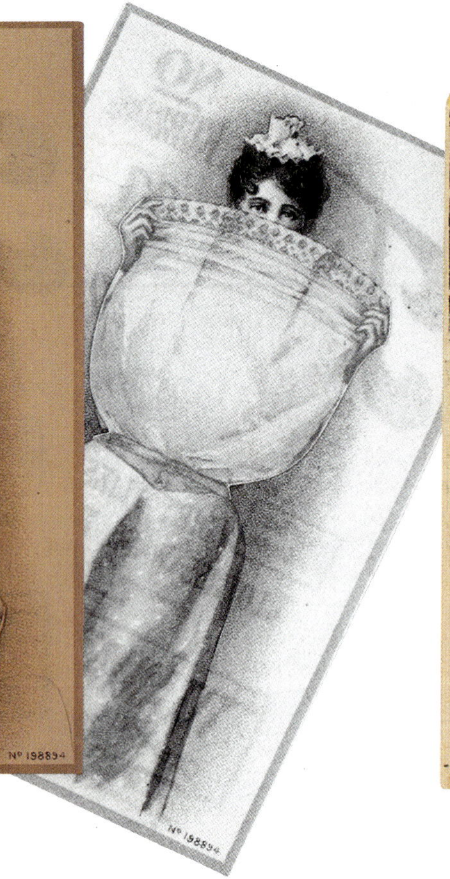

The Laundry

Even with the aid of the most up-to-date machines, wringers and dryers, 'washing at home is an exasperating business unless everyone engaged in it gets up early, say at 5 a.m. on Monday', wrote a lady signing herself 'Domestic Cat' in *The Lady*. 'Then the worst of the nuisance is over by noon, and the household work so forward that a dozen people might come in to afternoon tea and find the mistress serene, the maid spruce and the kettle boiling.'

The soap jelly should have been prepared on the previous Saturday, unless one of the ready-made brands was purchased. The family's linen was collected on that day, 'when all the dirty parts, such as necks, wrists, and children's drawers and pinafores', were well soaped and rubbed, and put into a tub or tray to soak till Monday.

An ingenious method of drying men's stiff collars was to put them while still damp around old cake tins covered with calico. In this way the collars would keep their shape.

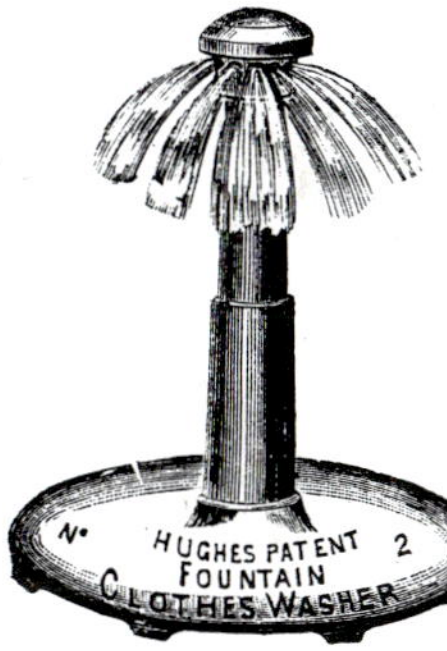

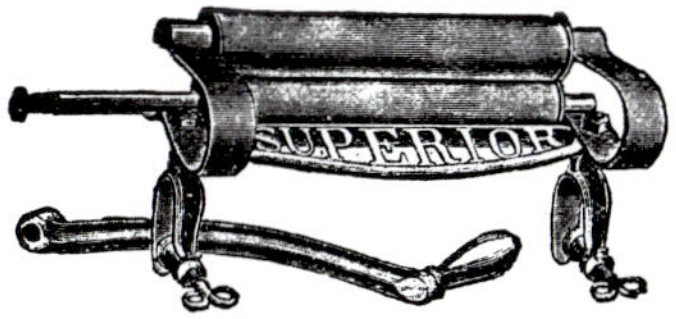

No. M30a. CLOTHES WRINGERS.

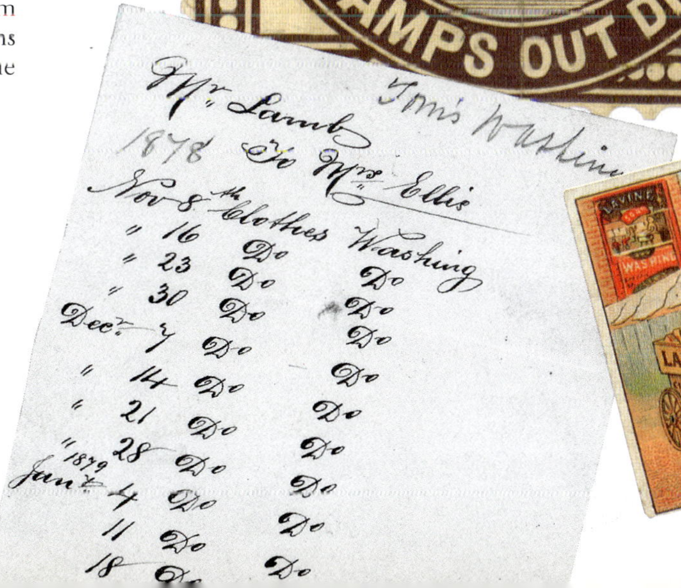

Mr. Lamb
Tom's Washing
1878 To Mrs Ellis
Nov 8th Clothes Washing
" 16 Do Do
" 23 Do Do
" 30 Do Do
Decr 7 Do Do
" 14 Do Do
" 21 Do Do
" 28 Do Do
1879 Jany 4 Do Do
11 Do Do
18 Do Do

IRONING & MENDING

ABOVE: Cotton-reel labels.

WEDNESDAY WAS the day for mangling and ironing; 'When Thursday's come, the week's work's done', as the saying went.

The process of mangling, which consisted of passing articles between weighted wooden rollers, 'is confined to sheets, towels, table-linen, and similar articles, which are without folds or plaits', wrote Mrs Beeton. 'Ironing is necessary to smooth body-linen, and made-up

IRON STANDS.
Cast, with Bright Face.
Common. 1/9, Best. 2/3 per doz.

IRON STANDS.
Cast, with Bright Face, and Wood Handle.
Per doz. 2/6

IRONS, CHARCOAL BOX.
With Side Bent Pipe.
5½, 6, 6½, 7, 7½, 8 inches
1/7, 1/7, 1/8, 1/8, 1/11, 1/11 each.
Joyce's Patent Fuel for ditto.
In sacks of 2 bushels ... each 2/10
-/4 each allowed for Sacks when returned.

articles of delicate texture or gathered into folds.' She went on to describe the common flat iron, the oval iron, the box iron, 'which is hollow, and heated by a red-hot iron inserted into the box', and the Italian iron. The whiteness could be restored to a scorched article with a mixture of vinegar, fuller's earth, dried fowls' dung, soap and the juice of two large onions.

Before the washing was put away, any mending had to be attended to. 'Experience alone can teach where the darning should begin and where it should end. Nothing is easier, indeed, than so to mend a hole in a stocking as that two or more are formed in its stead.' 'It is a good plan to run the heels of new stockings, or to fell a piece of tape flat on the seam of the heel. Buttons should always be sewn on with strong thread. Keep a piece of wax in your work-basket to rub on your thread and strengthen it', went another suggestion.

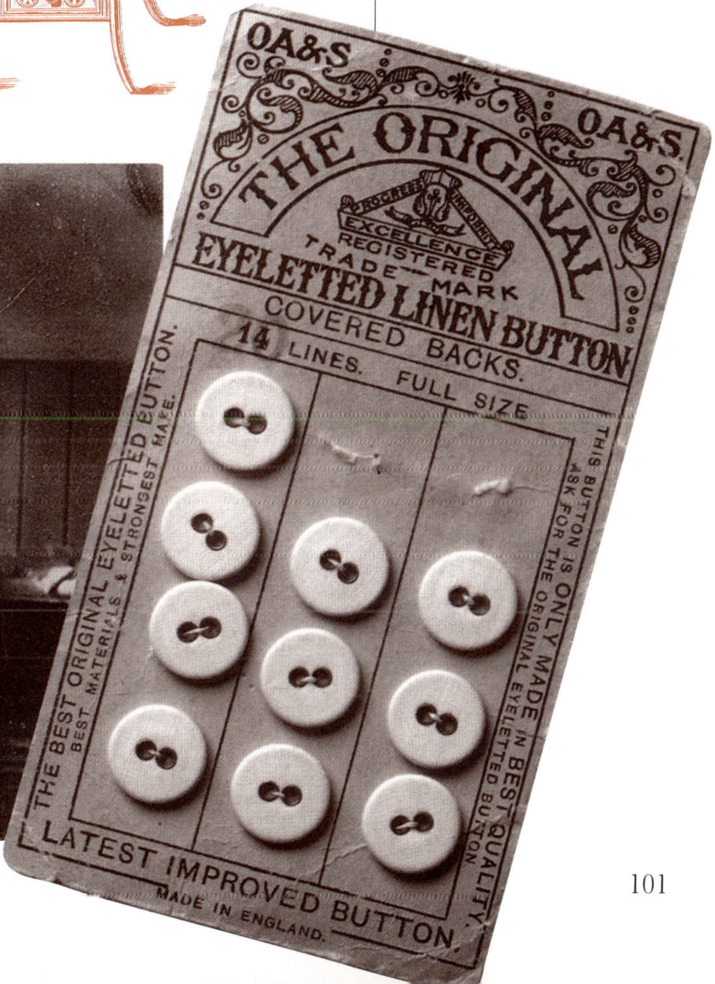

Dyeing & Refurbishing

Chemical dyes introduced a new and astonishing range of tints with which to colour fabrics. The dyeing might either be done at home, or the clothes and furnishings could be sent off to a dye works, which often doubled as a dry cleaner, another Victorian innovation.

The booklet distributed by Stevenson Bros. extolled the virtue of their dyeing methods which could 'restore temporarily spoiled articles to their original beauty and worth at a trifling cost' and 'damaged or faded articles could be changed to a hue that was rich and permanent'. They would happily dye to order household drapings, curtains, table covers and decorative hangings in silk, wool or cotton, damask, rep, tapestry or Roman satin.

Dyeing & Refurbishing

Advising on home dyeing, *The Lady* ran a series of articles in 1889, stating, 'the fair sex possess an unlimited stock of what, for want of a better name, we will term rubbish, such as ribbons, bows, sashes, gloves, stockings, mittens etc. which are too good to throw away, and yet are too much faded, stained or soiled to be of any use in their present condition.' These could be transformed by careful dyeing, and 'in the event of a non-success attending the first effort, the loss would be small'.

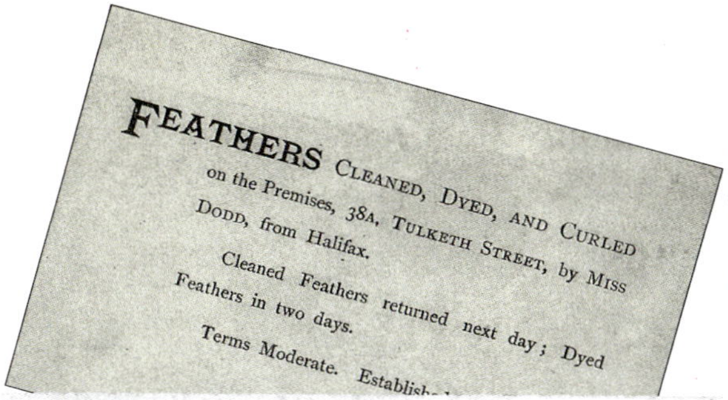

FEATHERS CLEANED, DYED, AND CURLED on the Premises, 38A, TULKETH STREET, by MISS DODD, from Halifax.

Cleaned Feathers returned next day; Dyed Feathers in two days.

Terms Moderate. Establish...

BELOW: A postcard given away by the Bury St Edmunds agent of P. & P. Campbell, the Perth Dye Works.

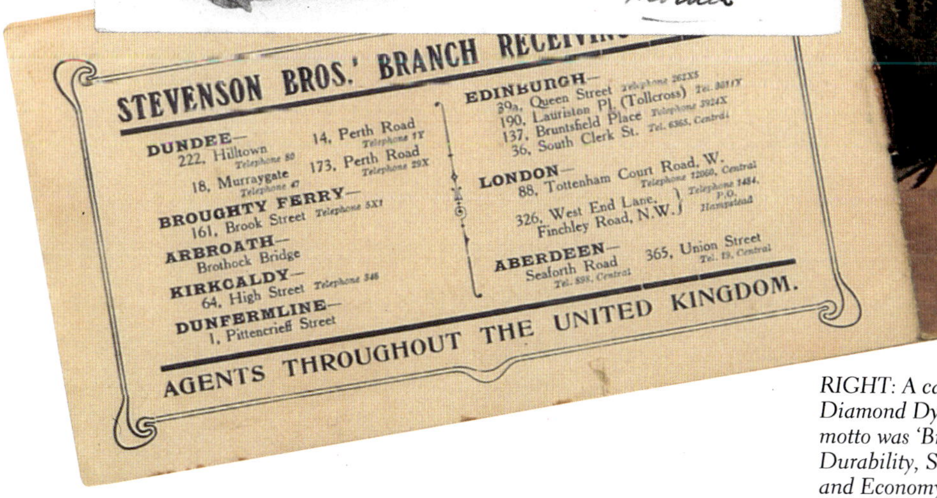

STEVENSON BROS.' BRANCH RECEIVING...

DUNDEE— 222, Hilltown *Telephone 80*; 14, Perth Road *Telephone 1Y*; 18, Murraygate *Telephone 47*; 173, Perth Road *Telephone 29X*	EDINBURGH— 39a, Queen Street *Telephone 262X5*; 190, Lauriston Pl. (Tollcross) *Tel. 3011Y*; 137, Bruntsfield Place *Telephone 3924X*; 36, South Clerk St. *Tel. 6365, Central*
BROUGHTY FERRY— 161, Brook Street *Telephone 5X1*	LONDON— 88, Tottenham Court Road, W. *Telephone 12060, Central*; 326, West End Lane, Finchley Road, N.W. *Telephone 3484, P.O. Hampstead*
ARBROATH— Brothock Bridge	ABERDEEN— Seaforth Road *Tel. 898, Central*; 365, Union Street *Tel. 19, Central*
KIRKCALDY— 64, High Street *Telephone 346*	
DUNFERMLINE— 1, Pittencrieff Street	

AGENTS THROUGHOUT THE UNITED KINGDOM.

RIGHT: A card for Diamond Dyes. Their motto was 'Brilliancy, Durability, Simplicity and Economy'.

Household Accounts

In well-regulated households one morning a week was devoted to the accounts. In this way improvements in domestic economy might be achieved and the master assisted in living within his means.

The diligent housekeeper noted every single item of expenditure in an account book, 'down to the last penny paid to the crossing sweeper'. Printed account books obtained from the stationer listed the classes of expenditure on the left-hand page: baker, butcher, poulterer, fishmonger, cheesemonger, tallow chandler, wood and coal,

RIGHT: The coinage of the Victorian period shown on a humorous Christmas card.

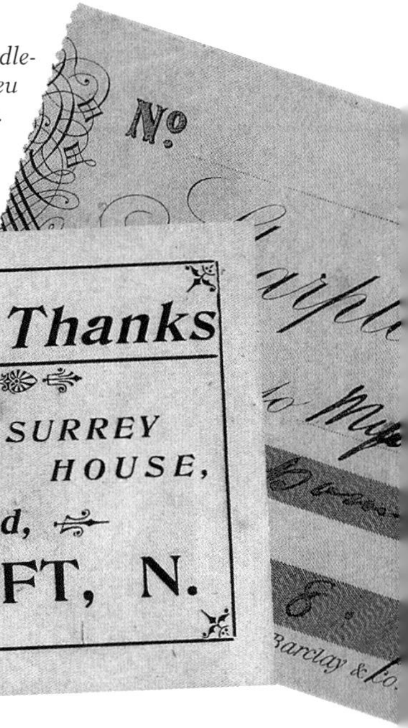

BELOW: A needle-book given in lieu of small change.

medicines, stationery and stamps, travelling expenses, wages, wearing apparel, charities.

Butchers' bills required especially careful weekly supervision, as errors in weight, even of ounces, or price, even of farthings, amounted to a considerable sum in the course of a year.

Included in the account books were ready reckoners and tables, including standard cab fares (London, 1853, by carriage with four or two wheels drawn by one horse: sixpence a mile within a radius of four miles from Charing Cross).

If the mistress of the house went out herself to pay the bills, she was advised to take with her a commonplace book in which to record receipts or any other useful household hints that might reach her ears.

Bills were to be receipted in ink, and on payments of over £2 no receipt was legal that was not accompanied by a penny stamp, supplied by the payee. The penalty for affixing a stamp without cancelling it was £10.

BELOW: A page from The Housekeeper's Memorandum Book, *'adapted for commencing the Account at any period of the year'.*

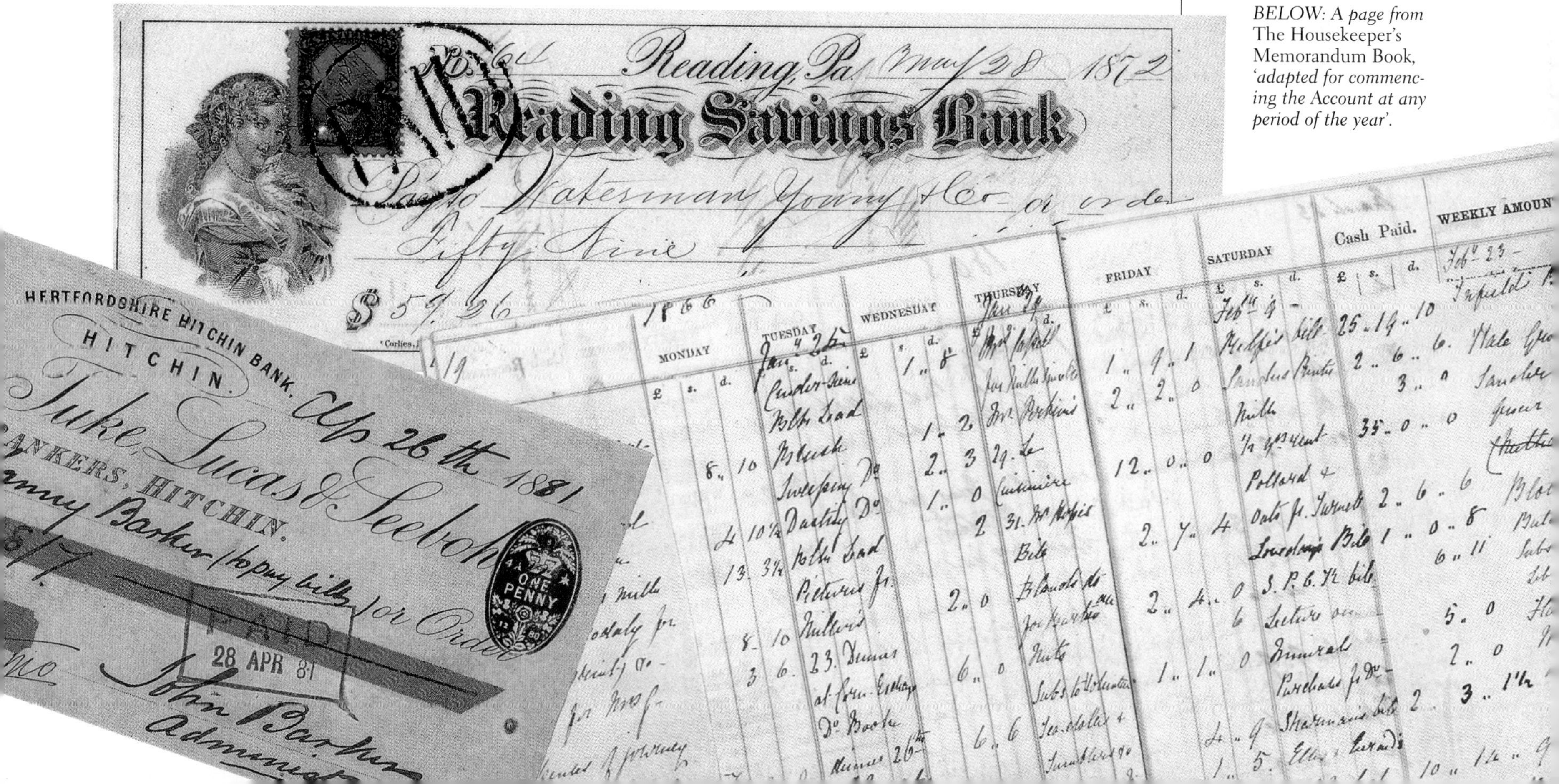

The Kitchen

Mrs Haweis, in a chapter entitled 'Homes for the Happy', described the essentials of a good kitchen. It should be 'a light airy room, where in every corner it is possible to see what one is doing (quite possible below the ground-line, as above it), where there are a good range for cooking, either portable or fixed, a table, a dresser for plates above, pots and pans below, and big

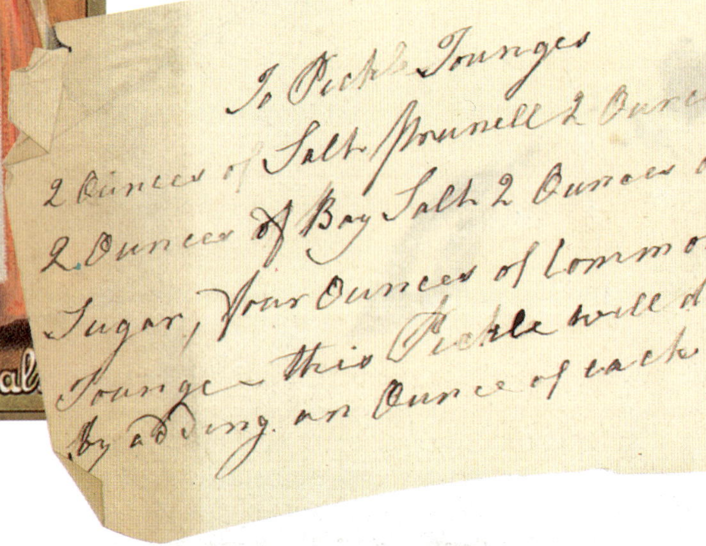
To Pickle Tounges
2 Ounces of Salt Prunell 2 Ounces of
2 Ounces of Bay Salt 2 Ounces of
Sugar, Four Ounces of Common
Tounge – this Pickle will do
by adding an Ounce of each

drawers for dusters and sundries.' As well as the main kitchen table, which was thoroughly scrubbed each day to produce a clean, whitened surface, another smaller one was often provided for dishing up.

A reliable clock was a necessity. The best position for this was over the mantelpiece, where the cook could consult it without turning away from the fire. The floor was often tiled or stone-flagged; a wooden floor generally had a covering of linoleum in an attempt to keep the kitchen free from vermin. Ordinary glazed tiles served as a good wall-covering, or else a varnished paper, usually buff in colour.

Mrs Beeton admonished cooks and kitchen maids to dress suitably: 'the modern crinoline is absurd, dangerous, out of place and extravagant', she wrote in 1869, liable to scorch and wear into holes. In the kitchen she advised that crinolines were 'useless incumbrances'.

THE KITCHEN

LEFT: The cover from a Leibig Company cookery book.

SPIRIT BOTTLES
With Screw Stoppers.

Kitchen Utensils

Weights and scales (the most important utensil in Mrs Beeton's view, as nothing had a more harmful influence on food than incorrect quantities), a pasteboard, rolling pin and paste cutters, a water filter, mincing machine, apple corer, soup strainer and vegetable cutter for cutting carrots and turnips in different shapes for soups and garnishing: these and a variety of iron and copper pots, pans and kettles, knives, saws and choppers, were the everyday requisites of the cook.

The authors of *Warne's Model Cookery* went on a tour of London's manufacturing and furnishing ironmongers to inspect their wares before making recommendations of kitchen equipment to the young and inexperienced housekeeper.

The newest and most fashionable jelly moulds, the Alexandra and the Brunswick Star, produced shapes with an opaque interior seen through a transparent outer jelly. The highest accolade for usefulness went to Captain Warren's Everybody's Cooking Pot, in which meat was cooked in an inner saucepan 'by means of *heat only*, without being touched by any liquid, save its own juices, or even wetted by steam.'

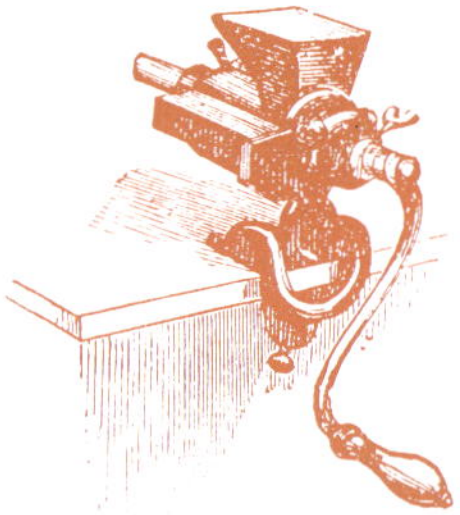

Kitchen Utensils

"COMPETITION GUIDE"
FOR THE
IRONMONGERY AND HARDWARE TRADES,
PUBLISHED BY
G. HARDING & SONS,
25, 27, 31, 33 & 35, LONG LANE, BOROUGH,
LONDON, S.E.

Telegraphic Address: "TIN WORKS, LONDON. Telephone No. 4689. Postal Address, "LONDON, S.E."
(Copyright and entered at Stationers' Hall.)

NOVEMBER 28TH, 1890.—No. 14. **SPECIAL NET PRICES.**

o. 233. CAKE HOOPS.
Strong.
, 7, 8, 10, 12 inches.
-, 6/-, 7/6, 9/-, 10/6 per doz.

CAKE PANS.
Plain Round. Deep Pattern.
No. 235. Common.
4, 5, 6, 7, 8, 9, 10,
2/-, 2/6, 3/6, 4/6, 6/-, 7/, 8/-,
11, 12 inches.
9/-, 10/- per doz.

No. 237. Strong.
5, 6, 7, 8, 9, 10, 10, 10 inches,
4/3, 5/-,5/9,7/3,8/9,11/9,15/-19/- per doz.
With Loose Bottoms 1/6 per doz. extra.

Our Manufactories, Offices, Show Rooms and Warehouses are close to the BOROUGH STATION of the CITY AND SOUTH LONDON ELECTRIC RAILWAY.

—:o:—

KE PANS.
Shallow Pattern.
Common.
0, 9, 10, 11,
5/6, 6/6, 7/6, 8/6,
hes.
r doz.

Common.
Four.
doz. Nests 10/-

rong.
9, 10,
, 8/3, 11/3,
doz.
doz. extra.

No. 237b. CAKE PANS.
Fluted Round.
Nos. 1, 2, 3, 4, 5, 6, 7.
4, 4½, 4¾, 5½, 5¾, 5¾, 6¼ inches.
5/-, 6/-, 7/-, 8/-, 9/-, 10/6 12/- per doz.

"VICTORIA"
SANDWICH OR JELLY
CAKE PLATES.
8, 9 inches.
1/3, 1/6 per doz.

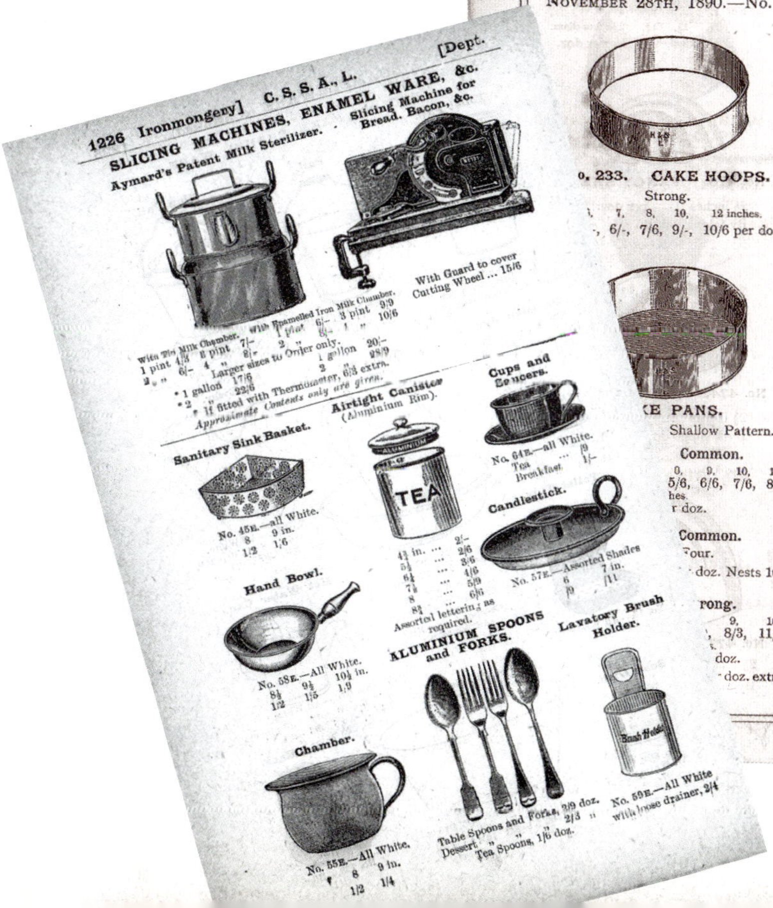

1226 Ironmongery] C. S. S. A., L. [Dept.

SLICING MACHINES, ENAMEL WARE, &c.

Aymard's Patent Milk Sterilizer.

With Tin Milk Chamber.
1 pint 4/3 3 pint 7/-
2 " 6/- 4 " 8/-
*1 gallon 17/6
*2 " 22/6

With Enamelled Iron Milk Chamber.
1 pint 6/- 3 pint 9/9
1½ " 6/- 4 " 10/6
2 " ...
1 gallon 20/-
2 " 28/9

Larger sizes to Order only.
* If fitted with Thermometer, 6/3 extra.
Approximate Contents only are given.

Slicing Machine for Bread, Bacon, &c.
With Guard to cover Cutting Wheel ... 15/6

Sanitary Sink Basket.
No. 45E.—all White.
8 9 in.
1/2 1/6

Airtight Canister (Aluminium Rim).
4½ in. ... 2/-
5½ ... 2/6
6¼ ... 3/6
7⅛ ... 4/6
8 ... 5/9
8¾ ... 6/6
Assorted lettering as required.

Cups and Saucers.
No. 64E.—all White.
Tea ... /9
Breakfast 1/-

Candlestick.
No. 57E.—Assorted Shades
6 7 in.
/9 /11

Hand Bowl.
No. 58E.—All White.
8½ 9½ 10½ in.
1/2 1/5 1/9

ALUMINIUM SPOONS and FORKS.
Table Spoons and Forks, 2/9 doz.
Dessert " " 2/3 "
Tea Spoons, 1/6 doz.

Lavatory Brush Holder.
No. 59E.—All White with loose drainer, 2/4

Chamber.
No. 55E.—All White.
8 9 in.
1/2 1/4

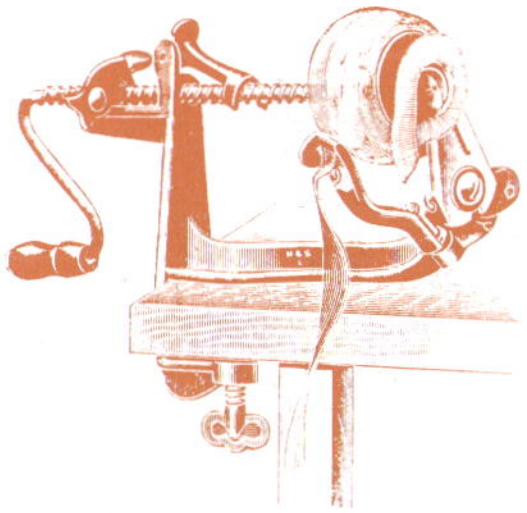

APPLE CORERS.
The "Little Star."
Each 3/-

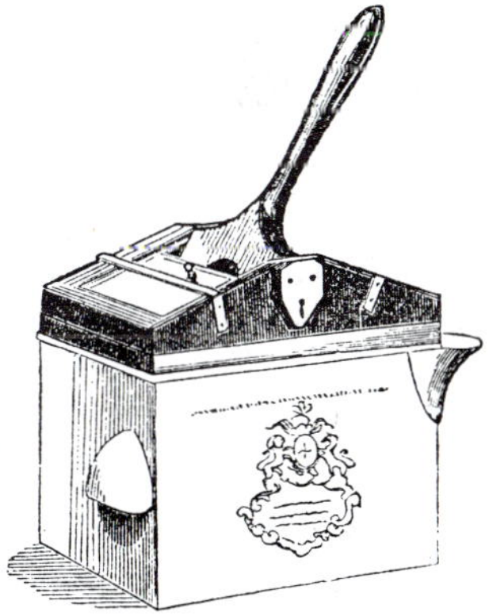

Kent's Patent Soup Strainer.

The Larder

The room or cupboard used for fresh, uncooked food such as meat and fish, and dishes ready prepared for the table – and scraps returned from the table as well – 'should have a northerly aspect, to ensure coolness, and must be dry, light, well ventilated, and scrupulously clean', as described in *Household Hints*. 'The ceiling and walls (if not tiled) should be well limewashed at least once a year. The shelves should, if possible, be of slate; failing this, they must be well scrubbed weekly. . . The windows, if not of perforated zinc gauze (which is best) should be opened constantly, a sheet of fine muslin being stretched taut, across the window, to keep out flies, &c.'

'If possible, the floor should be of stone, but in any case there must be a slab of slate for the fish, and one for the milk, which must be kept well away from anything likely to taint it.' In towns, the larder was probably a dark cupboard, 'agreeably disposed between the main drain and the dusthole; still, careful cleanliness and attention will do a great deal with even this unpromising hole'.

STOVES & COOKERS

IN 1889 MRS HAWEIS stated quite categorically, 'The comfort of the whole house lies largely with the kitchen range.' The best, in her experience, 'the cheapest in the end, and cleanest as well as simplest, is the "Leamington" range, built by Stevens'.

GAS STOVES OR HOT PLATES.

The "Ideal."

19 × 8½ inches ... ... each 11/-

STOVE BRUSHES.

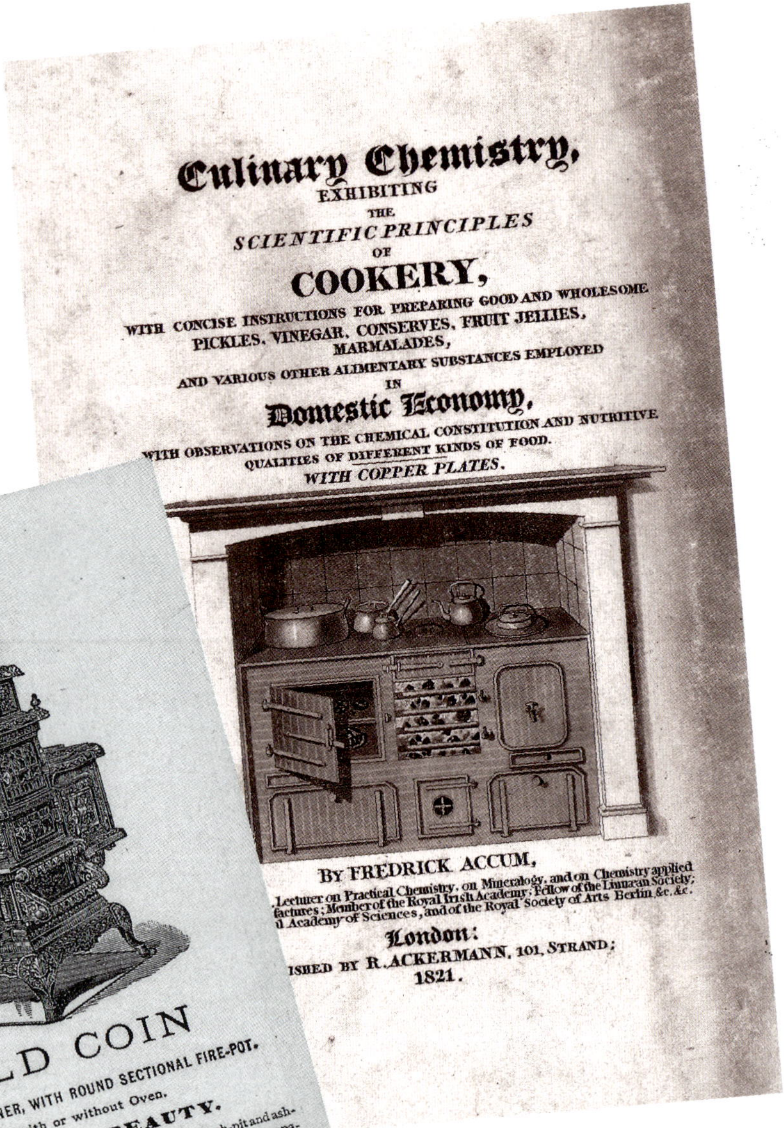

Culinary Chemistry,

EXHIBITING

THE

SCIENTIFIC PRINCIPLES

OF

COOKERY,

WITH CONCISE INSTRUCTIONS FOR PREPARING GOOD AND WHOLESOME PICKLES, VINEGAR, CONSERVES, FRUIT JELLIES, MARMALADES,

AND VARIOUS OTHER ALIMENTARY SUBSTANCES EMPLOYED IN

Domestic Economy,

WITH OBSERVATIONS ON THE CHEMICAL CONSTITUTION AND NUTRITIVE QUALITIES OF DIFFERENT KINDS OF FOOD.

WITH COPPER PLATES.

BY FREDRICK ACCUM,

Lecturer on Practical Chemistry, on Mineralogy, and on Chemistry applied ...factures; Member of the Royal Irish Academy; Fellow of the Linnaean Society; ...l Academy of Sciences, and of the Royal Society of Arts Berlin, &c. &c.

London:

...ISHED BY R. ACKERMANN, 101, STRAND;

1821.

Mrs Beeton was of the same opinion, the advantages of it being so great 'that an inexperienced cook would scarcely fail to serve up a passable dinner if she had a "Leamington" at her disposal; whilst the same person, with an open range, would have acquitted herself in a wretched manner'. The Leamington kitchen range had won first prize and a medal at the Great Exhibition in 1851.

The closed range combined ovens for baking and roasting and a boiler supplying hot water with hot plates on top for boiling and steaming; 'the old-fashioned, troublesome habit of roasting with a jack has nearly ceased from the land.'

Gas appliances were first used as a means of keeping the food and the plates warm. In small or airless kitchens, where in summer the heat generated by the 'iron monsters' became insupportable, they were sometimes employed as an auxiliary means of cooking, but only for families of moderate size.

BELOW: An American stove burning coal and wood.

The Ice Safe

NINETEENTH-CENTURY American visitors to Britain bemoaned the lack of iced drinking water, and it was from America that the ideas came for the new-fangled freezers, ice safes, ice caves and refrigerators. As the demand for ice grew, icebergs from Canada and Norway were towed across the Atlantic. 'Ice, once a luxury enjoyed only by the rich, has become a necessity of daily life.' So stated *Warne's Model Housekeeper*, which suggested storing ice in a pocket of woollen cloth stuffed with feathers or a double-cased wooden chest for the dining room with a charcoal infilling to cool the wine. The economy of keeping butter fresh and fish good was clearly worth the 1d or 2d per lb that the ice cost.

No. 17.– OVAL MELON.

7 inches long, 18*s.* 9*d.* each.

BELOW: A page from The Book of Ices by *A. B. Marshall.*

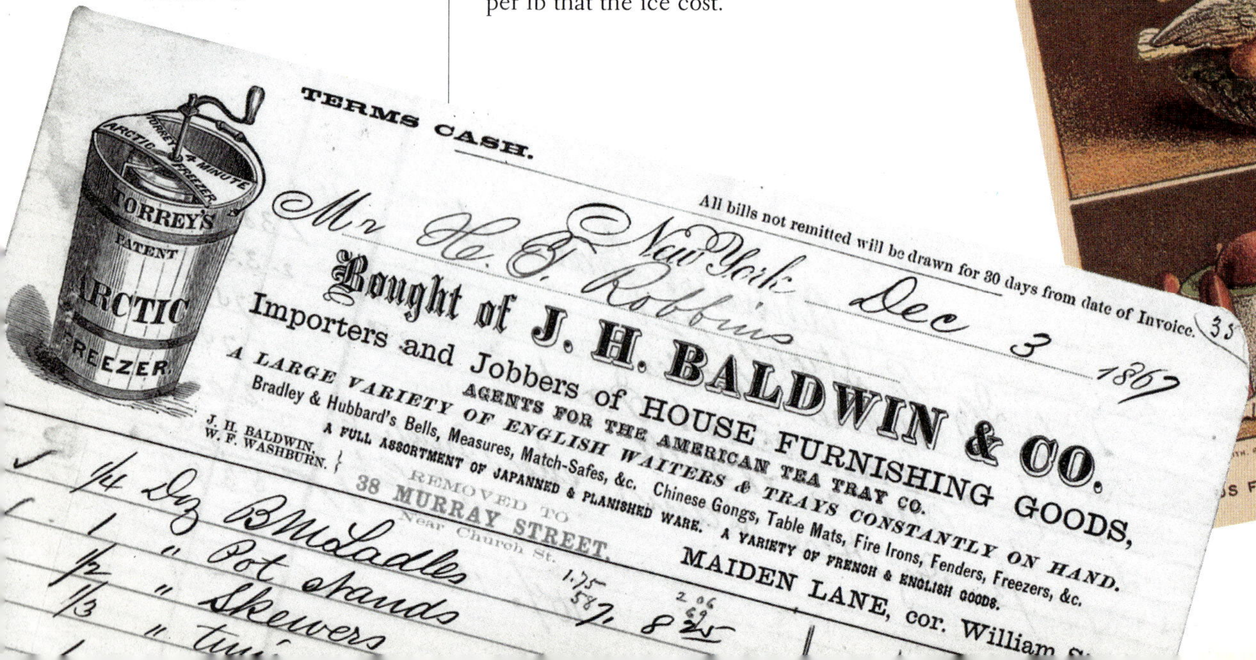

TERMS CASH.

TORREY'S PATENT ARCTIC FREEZER

ARCTIC TORREY'S 4 MINUTE FREEZER

New York Dec 3 1867

All bills not remitted will be drawn for 30 days from date of Invoice.

35

Mr H. E. Robbins

Bought of J. H. BALDWIN & CO.

Importers and Jobbers of HOUSE FURNISHING GOODS,

AGENTS FOR THE AMERICAN TEA TRAY CO.

A LARGE VARIETY OF ENGLISH WAITERS & TRAYS CONSTANTLY ON HAND.

Bradley & Hubbard's Bells, Measures, Match-Safes, &c. Chinese Gongs, Table Mats, Fire Irons, Fenders, Freezers, &c.

A FULL ASSORTMENT OF JAPANNED & PLANISHED WARE. A VARIETY OF FRENCH & ENGLISH GOODS.

J. H. BALDWIN, W. F. WASHBURN.

REMOVED TO 38 MURRAY STREET, Near Church St.

MAIDEN LANE, cor. William St.

1/4 Doz BM Ladles 1.75

1 " Pot stands 587 2.06

1/2 " Skewers 69

1/3 " twi... 8 25

The appetite for iced dishes increased prodigiously: cream ices, sorbets, mousses, and iced savouries such as Soufflé of Curry à la Ripon. Frederick Vine, the author of *Ices: Plain and Decorated*, gave many receipts for these 'ethereal dainties', such as Trophy à la Britannique, requiring moulds in the form of a bombe, a lion and Britannia to be filled with a combination of redcurrant and green grape water ice, and chocolate and vanilla cream. Other 'artistic freezings' included a Trophy Glace à l'Amour, a cucumber-shaped mould filled with greengage water ice with a delectable centre of lemon cream.

The Ice Safe

No. 19.—BASKET OF FRUITS.

Very handsome. 3 pints, 26s. each.

LEFT: A page from The Book of Ices *showing moulds for ice puddings. The moulds were sold at Marshall's School of Cookery in Cavendish Square in London.*

THE SCULLERY & PANTRY

BELOW: Brooke's soap described itself as 'The world's most marvellous Cleanser and Polisher'.

NOTHING DISMAYED the young husband so much, it was claimed in *The Young Lady's Book,* as plate that was scratched, handles broken from jugs, glasses severed from their stems, the blades of knives notched and with their handles discoloured and loose, and the drains stopped with dusters and tea-cloths. In the scullery and pantry, as elsewhere in the house, there was a right way of doing everything.

The Scullery & Pantry

In the scullery the plates and dishes, and the various utensils used in the kitchen, were washed. It was also the proper place for cleaning and preparing fish and vegetables. In the pantry the glass, plate and cutlery were cleaned and polished, knife-cleaning machines in due course replacing the traditional leather-covered knifeboard. The best plate-rags were said to be those made from the tops of old cotton stockings, soaked and boiled in a mixture of fresh milk and hartshorn powder.

'To clean glass bottles or decanters which are very stained, use stinging-nettles and hot water, pressing the nettles into the bottle and shaking until the stains have disappeared and the glass is clear and bright', ran a useful hint for the servants responsible for this. 'Raw potato cut into small pieces is also good.'

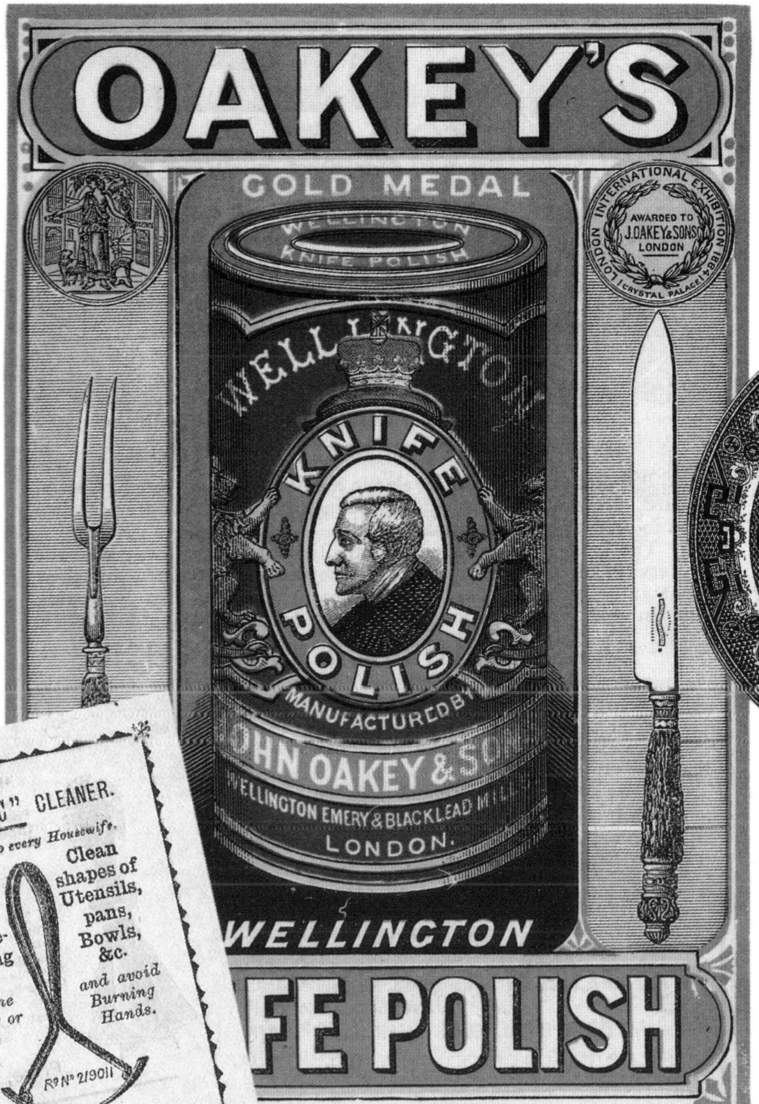

Leathers are RUBBER BACKED.

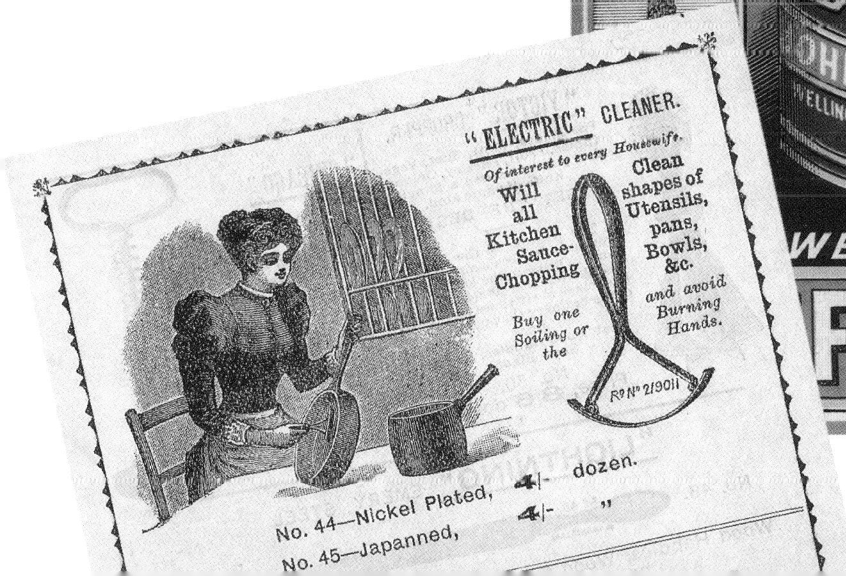

The Store Cupboard

A STORE CUPBOARD reserved for dry goods was a necessity for the smooth running of any household and for the practice of sound domestic economy. In *Warne's Model Cookery* it was remarked that 'The trouble of housekeeping is much diminished by having a fixed day for giving out to the cook the tea, sugar, coffee, plums, &c., which are likely to be required during the coming week; weighing out the quantities in proportion to the number of the family. Every week she should account for these quantities, bringing back whatever may chance to remain over and above her use.'

The monthly grocery list prepared by Mrs Haweis included flour, sugar, Rangoon and Patna rice, Scotch barley, treacle, arrowroot, mushroom ketchup, Harvey and Worcester sauce, fish sauce ('very small bottle'), curry powder and baking powder.

The cupboard typically contained 'earthenware jars for sugars, and tins for keeping tea, coffee and biscuits. The large or small tins in which biscuits are sold should be retained for these uses.'

Lemons were purchased for keeping in June or July, when they were cheapest, and hung in separate netted bags; tallow candles were purchased in March as they kept best when made in cold weather; unroasted coffee was more economical than roasted coffee: 'there is a roaster (peculiar to Ireland) which is turned over the fire like a mop, that anyone can use with ease.'

Household Nuisances

The housekeeper had to wage intelligent and ceaseless war against bugs and fleas, as at any moment a stray parent might be brought into the house from cab, omnibus or train. 'Houses for the Happy' was the heading of the chapter on pest extermination in *The Art of Housekeeping* from the pen of Mrs Haweis. Blackbeetles and vermin were the result of dirty, wasteful habits and stupid neglect; a visit to the kitchen at night might reveal to the mistress carelessness on the part of the servants and beetles' delight in the form of dregs of beer, tea leaves and half-scoured bones from the *pot au feu*. Against moths she recommended camphor balls or Russian leather parings, and against flies muslin nailed across windows adjacent to 'low' streets.

Lucifer matches, Mrs Balfour assured her readers, were the greatest cause of accidents, with 'hundreds of lives lost, multitudes brought to ruin and thousands of pounds' worth of property sacrificed' by throwing them about carelessly. Avoid panic, she stressed, warning 'women should try not to scream'.

Fig. 19.

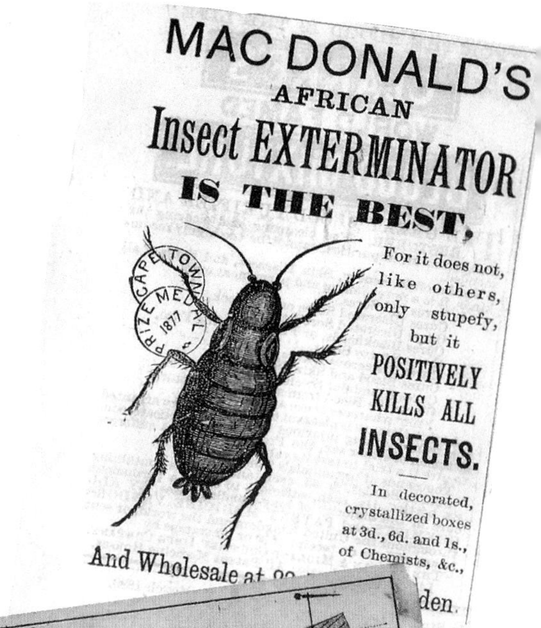

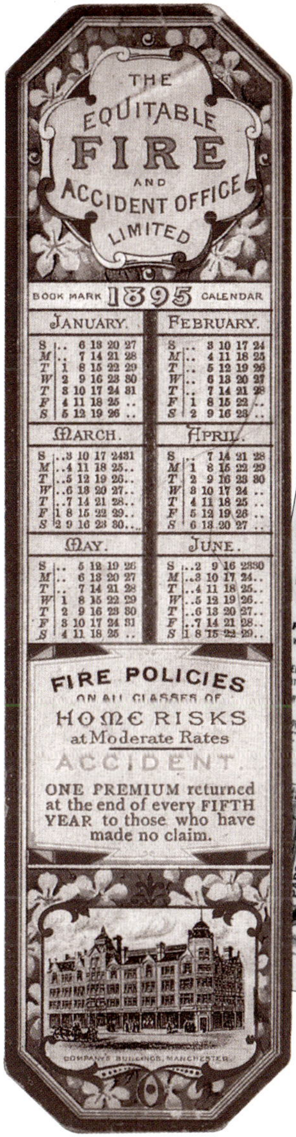

Household Nuisances

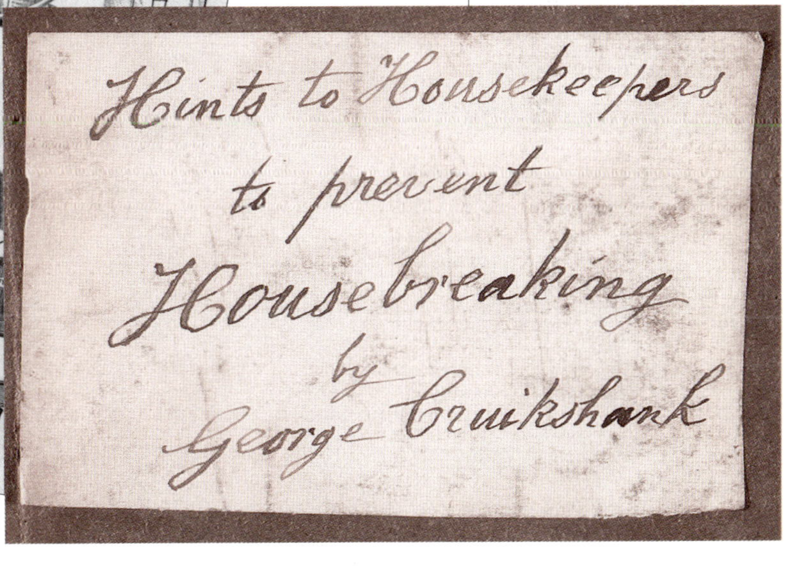

The Back Door

The back door was the threshold to the domestic quarters. It was to this door, the tradesmen's entrance, that deliveries were made and the dustman, chimney-sweep, knife-grinder and chair-mender called. The servants returned to the back door on their Sundays out, and it was from here that their 'followers' were discouraged.

The cook was 'the doorkeeper'. In *The Art of Housekeeping, A Bridal Garland,* Mrs Haweis warned of the time that might be wasted by the cook if sensible standing orders were not made with tradesmen on a regular basis. She described 'harpies', touting at the back door for business, 'hasty guesswork in calculating what will be required, and the errands that will keep the cook talking, whilst the back door is on the latch, or open to every passer-by'. That cooks could be bribed by tradesmen selling wares at the back door was, Mrs Haweis regretted, a widespread system, 'encouraging dishonest servants and corrupting honest ones'.

It was important not to forget that the purveyor was the servant of the consumer, and the butcher who sent short weight or the grocer and draper making small mistakes to their own advantage 'should not be reasoned with, but quitted'. If arrangements could be made directly with producers, for example a farmer rearing poultry in the country, that was most beneficial to both parties. One back-door trade that was disapproved of, but considered an inevitable perquisite of the cook, was her sale of 'wash'. This consisted of leftovers, vegetable peelings, tea-leaves, children's crusts and wine lees, for which she received the odd shillings and pence from the coster, 'a nondescript man with a cart and donkey or miserable horse who will call every morning, early, with pails and barrels to remove it'.

The Back Door

LEFT: A baker delivering his loaves in Southgate in north London.

The Boot Room & The Cellar

The nether regions of a Victorian house might easily include among its offices a small space or room designated for the business of keeping boots and shoes clean, a much more laborious affair when the streets were dusty, muddy and constantly full of horse traffic. Many were the receipts for this task: castor oil for softening, milk for patent leather, spirits of wine for white satin

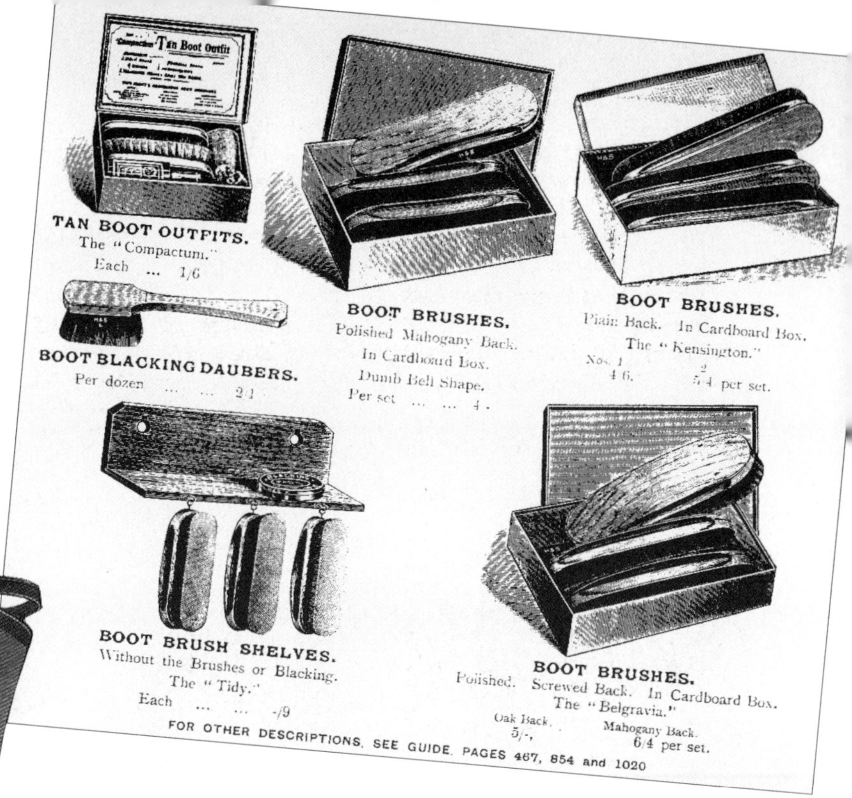

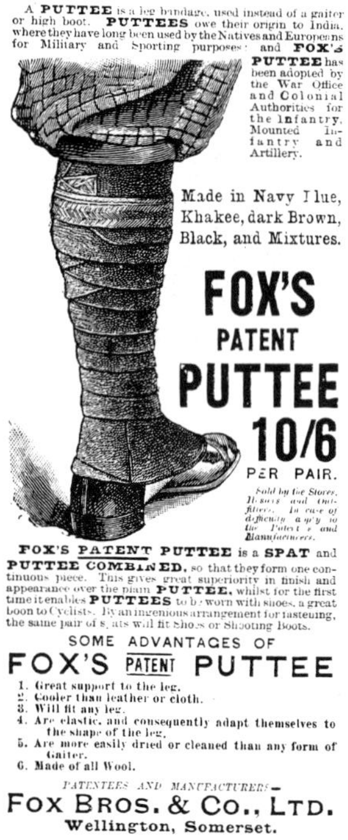

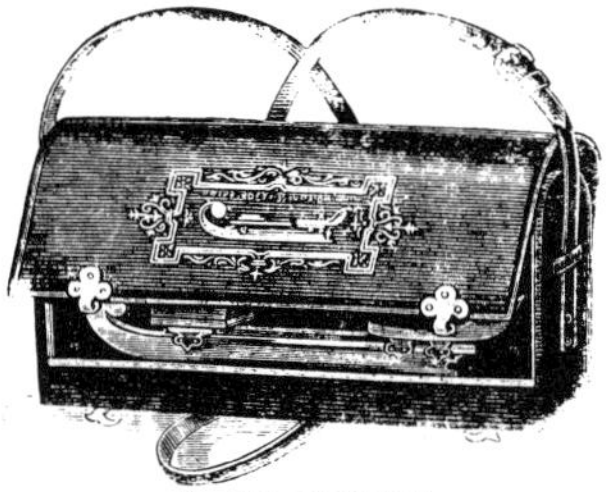

60.—Bag for Skates.

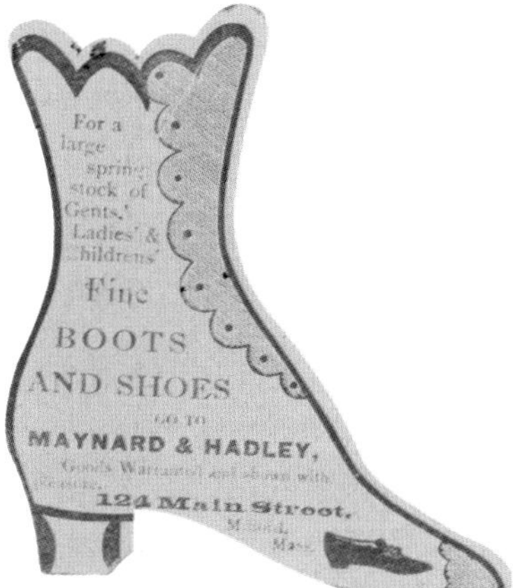

and a mixture of spermaceti oil, vinegar, treacle and finely-powdered ivory black for the very muddy boots. When considering a journey on a wet day, Burgundy pitch heated with beeswax and turpentine made good waterproofing.

Generally houses were still built with the provision of a cellar, although one expert spoke disparagingly of modern 'little poking wine-cellars, into which it is often difficult to get a hogshead', and emphasized that the space under the staircase was quite unsuitable, though it was better than putting wine next to the laundry flues. T.G. Greg affirmed in his book *Through a Glass Lightly*: 'Not to have a cellar is derogatory to the dignity of man. Yet it is notable that, while every petty clerk or budding draper clamours for a bathroom, not one in a thousand will insist upon his wine vault.' The perfect 'palace of the grape' should be deep, and a 'pattern of neatness, so that yourself can descend thereunto with pleasure, and conduct your friend with pride'.

Decanting the wine was usually done two or three hours before it was to be drunk. Patent devices were designed for this job, 'since very few possess the requisite steadiness of hand, with the eye ready to stop as soon as the sediment begins to move'. Adequate stock for a cellar would consist, Mr Shaw wrote in *Wine, the Vine and the Cellar*, of 'a few dozen of different kinds of port, sherry, claret, a little champagne with a few bottles of spirits'. For purchasing such, 'Avoid the advertising vintner as you would the Devil, and hie you only to that fine, old, crusted, long-matured variety – known as the Old Fashioned Wine Merchant.' 'Baser potables' such as stout should be kept apart from wine.

ESTABLISHED 1860. REBUILT 1881.

Bought of W. GIBSON,

WINE, SPIRIT AND BEER MERCHANT,

41, KEPPEL STREET, W.C.

GLN. | DOZ. | BOTS.

CHABLIS
CLARET
HOCK
PORT
SHERRY
SAUTERNE
CHAMPAGNE
BURGUNDY
BRANDY
GIN, SWEETENED
GIN, UNSWEETENED
HOLLANDS
WHISKY, IRISH
WHISKY, SCOTCH
LIQUEURS
ALLSOPP'S DINNER ALE
BASS & CO.'S PALE ALE
IND COOPE'S ROMFORD ALE
UNIVERSITY PALE ALE
LONDON STOUT
GUINNESS'S DUBLIN STOUT
LAGER BEER
CYDER
GINGER ALE
POTASS WATER
SODA WATER
BOTTLES
SYPHONS

MADEIRA
MARSALA
MOSELLE
RUM
LEMONADE
GINGER BEER
CASES

Decanter (Mes.).

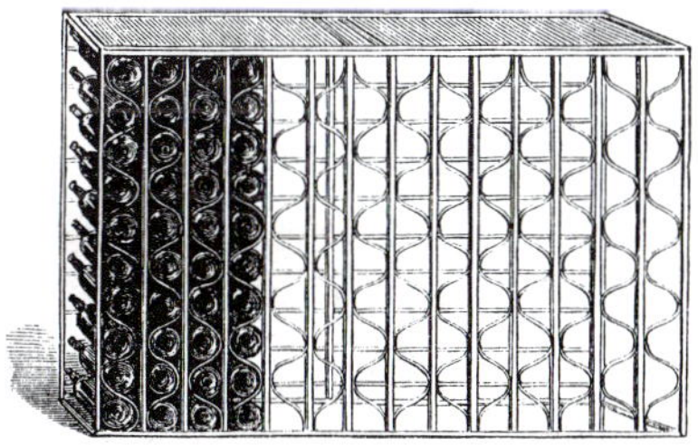

REGISTERED CELLULAR WINE BINS; REST FOR EACH BOTTLE. No. 2.

THE BOOT ROOM & THE CELLAR

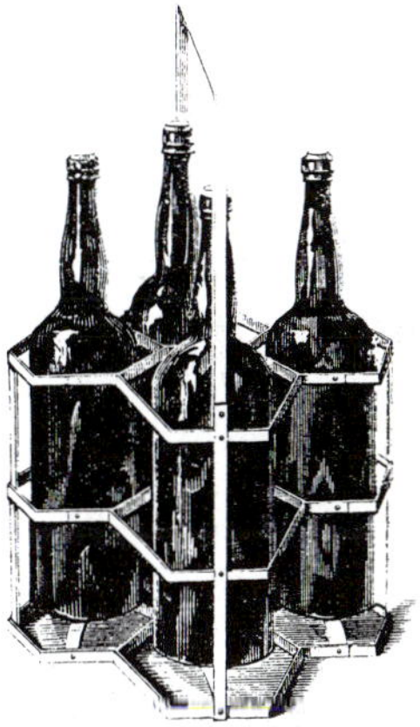

METAL BOTTLE-CARRIER.

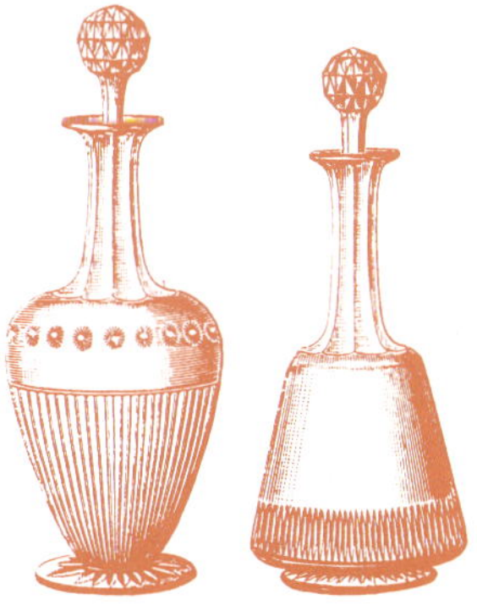

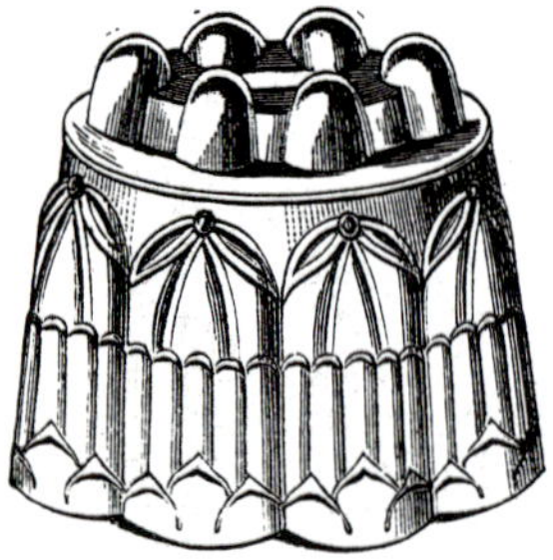

H 14. OVAL.

Nos. 1, 2, 3.
1, 1½, 2 pints.
18/-, 16/-, 18/- per doz.

THE ILLUSTRATIONS in this book fall mainly into the category of ephemera, 'minor transient documents of everyday life'. For the collector of ephemera, the Victorian household is a good subject in which to specialize. There is every expectation of making interesting and amusing discoveries, not only at fairs and sales, but also amongst the muddle of papers that so often survive their original owners.

Items may have been kept originally as a record or reminder – of how to re-order a favourite pair of gloves or a comfortable mattress, for example; of where the best tea set came from, of the name of a reliable plumber or trustworthy employment agency. Alternatively, they may have had a sentimental value as a memory of a happy time or place, or of a particular friendship.

It is just as likely that an item of ephemera – a scrap of paper or snippet – survives purely by chance, marking the page of a useful remedy or receipt in a book, for instance, or the point at which the reader lost interest. It might have fallen down behind a heavy piece of furniture that is never moved; it might have been pushed to the back of a drawer or left undisturbed underneath the lining paper (which might in itself be of interest), or been left in a work basket, writing box, coat pocket, suitcase or handbag.

Moving house, emptying attics and cupboards, and thinking of throwing away belongings that are out of fashion or have outlived their usefulness, almost always produces surprises, although it is becoming increasingly rare to find anything from as long ago as the nineteenth century. The fragments that turn up may have little in

About Ephemera

the way of monetary value, but they almost certainly tell us something about how things were done, and perhaps what things cost, at some earlier time. As this album shows, ephemera such as bills and account books, advertisements and trade brochures, postcards, greetings cards and calendars, menus and place cards of a century ago can provide intriguing details of how life was lived in a Victorian household. And they are a genuine link with the past.

If you require specific advice, or simply want more information about collecting ephemera, write to the Ephemera Society (enclosing a stamped, addressed envelope). Founded in London in 1975, its success has led to other ephemera societies being set up in America, Canada and Australia. In 1993 the world's first Centre for Ephemera Studies opened at the University of Reading, England. Its aim is to encourage the use of printed throwaways as material for the study of social and printing history.

The addresses of the various ephemera societies are as follows:

The Ephemera Society,
84 Marylebone High Street,
London W1M 3DE

The Ephemera Society of America Inc., P. O. Box 10, Schoharie, NY 12157

The Ephemera Society of Canada Inc., 36 Macauley Drive, Thornhill, Ontario, L3T 5S5

The Ephemera Society of Australia Inc., P. O. Box 479, Warraguil, Victoria 3820

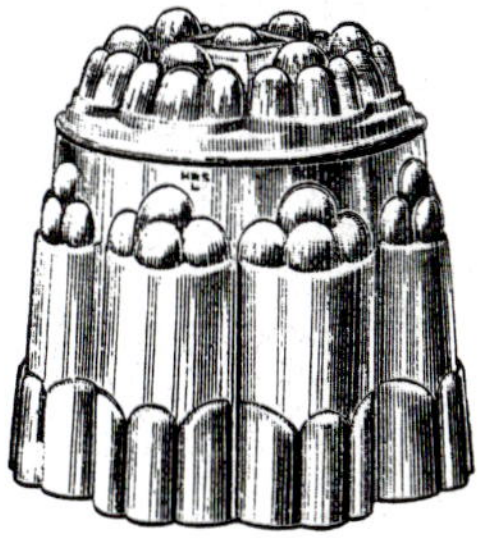

H 1. ROUND.
Nos. 1, 2, 3.
1, 1½, 2 pints.
Without pipe 16/-, 17/-, 18/- per doz.
With ,, 22/-, 23/-, 24/- ,,

Acknowledgements

The ephemera reproduced in this book is from the collection of Amoret Tanner, to whom Elizabeth Drury and Philippa Lewis are immensely grateful. The wallpapers reproduced on pages 11, 19, 53, 73 and 93 were printed in Islington by John Perry and Co. for Cole and Son, using the original Victorian woodblocks. The paintings on pages 42, 46, 48 and 96 are from the Bridgeman Art Library, and The Mansell Collection supplied images on pages 35 and 54.

Other illustrations, and quotations in the text, are from the following books: *The Architect's Compendium and Complete Catalogue* (London, 1895–1903); Balfour, Mrs Clara Lucas, *Homely Hints on Household Management* (London, n.d.); *The Ball Room Guide* (London, n.d.); Beaty-Pownall, S., *Household Hints* (London, 1910); Beeton, Mrs Isabella, *The Book of Household Management* (2nd edn., London, 1869); *Beeton's Ladies' Bazaar and Fancy-Fair Book* (London, n.d.); *The Best Way Book* (London, n.d.); Burbidge, F.W. *Domestic Floriculture* (Edinburgh and London, 1874); Campbell, Lady Colin, *Etiquette of Good Society* (London, Paris, New York and Melbourne, 1898); Clark, G.C., *Dinner Napkins and How to Fold Them* (London, n.d.); Cobbett, Anne, *The English Housekeeper* (London, 1842); Cooke, Rev. T., *The Universal Letter Writer* (Halifax, 1859); Eastlake, C.L., *Hints on Household Taste* (3rd edn., London, 1872); Edwards, Frederick, *Our Domestic Fire-Places: A Treatise on the Economical Use of Fuel and Prevention of Smoke* (London, 1865); *Good Things Made, Said and Done* (Leeds, 1888); Greg, T.G., *Through a Glass Lightly* (London, 1897); Hall, W.W., *How to Live Long, or Health Maxims Physical, Mental and Moral* (London, 1881); Harrison, Constance Cary, *Woman's Handiwork in Modern Homes* (London and New York, 1881); Haweis, Mrs H.R., *The Art of Decoration* (London, 1881); Haweis, Mrs H.R., *The Art of Beauty* (London, 1878); Haweis, Mrs H.R., *The Art of Housekeeping* (London, 1889); *Home Notes*, ed. 'Isobel', vol. II (London, 1894); Johnson, C.W., *Our House and Garden* (London, 1864); *The Lady* (London, 1885–1903); Loudon, Jane, *The Lady's Country Companion* (London, 1845); MacKarness, Mrs Henry, *The Young Lady's Book* (London, 1876); Maitland, A.C., *What Shall We Have for Breakfast?* (London, 1901); Mann, Robert J., *Domestic Economy and Household Science* (London, 1878); Marshall, A.B., *The Book of Ices* (London, 1857); Murphy, Shirley Foster, *Our Homes and How to Make Them Healthy* (London, Paris and New York, 1883); Muthesius, Hermann, *The English House* (trans. Janet Seligman, London, 1979, original edn, Berlin, 1904); O'Brien, Thomas & Co., *Illustrated Catalogue of Goods* (London, n.d.); Panton, Mrs J.E., *From Kitchen to Garret* (London, 1888); *Party-Giving on Every Scale* (London, 1882); Perkins, J., *Floral Designs for the Table* (London, 1877); Planche, Frederick d'Arros, *Guess Me* (London, n.d.); *The Popular Recreator*, vol. I (London, Paris and New York, n.d.); Riego de la Branchardière, Madame, *The Netting Book for Guipure d'Art* (London, 1868); Shaw, Thomas G., *Wine, the Vine and the Cellar* (London, 1863); *Social Etiquette* (London, 1860); Southgate, H., *Things a Lady Would Like to Know* (Edinburgh, 1878); Tuite, Eva, *Lemco Dishes for All Seasons* (London, n.d.); *Victorian Shopping, Harrod's Catalogue for 1895* (reprint, Newton Abbot, 1972); Vine, Fred T., *Ices: Plain and Decorated* (London and Glasgow, n.d.); Wadleigh, R.H., *Head-Gear, Antique and Modern* (Boston, 1879); *Waiting at Table* (London and New York, n.d.); *Warne's Etiquette of the Dinner-Table* (London, n.d.); *Warne's Model Cookery and Housekeeping Book* (London, 1869); *Warne's Model Housekeeper* (London, 1879); Williams, J., *The Footman's Guide* (London, n.d.); Young, Mrs H.M., *The Lemco Cookery Book* (London, 1897).